A
Woman's
Daily Prayer Book

Publications International, Ltd.

Nancy Parker Brummett is a freelance writer, columnist, and author of four books. She resides in Colorado Springs, Colorado. Leading women closer to the heart of God is the hallmark of her speaking and writing ministries. To learn more about her life and work, visit *www.nancyparkerbrummett.com.*

Christine A. Dallman is a freelance writer living near Everett, Washington. She is the author of *Daily Devotions for Seniors,* an inspirational resource for maturing adults, as well as coauthor of several other Publications International, Ltd., titles.

Louis Weber, CEO
Publications International, Ltd.
7373 North Cicero Avenue
Lincolnwood, Illinois 60712

Permission is never granted for commercial purposes.

ISBN-13: 978-1-4508-1522-2
ISBN-10: 1-4508-1522-7

Manufactured in China.

8 7 6 5 4 3 2 1

Library of Congress Control Number: 2010938852

Time for Prayer

The importance of prayer cannot be overstated. It is our lifeline to God. Sure, we can get by without it for a period of time, but we soon find ourselves feeling confused and overwhelmed. Trying to go it on our own may seem strong, but it is futile. If we get in the habit of prayer, we have peace of mind to head off any destructive feelings before they snowball.

Spiritual needs for nourishment and refreshment are very much like physical needs. Our hearts and minds can feel weary and worn from dealing with the "stuff" of life. Connecting with God through prayer brings spiritual renewal—like a shower for our soul and a meal for our spirit. Jesus himself, when he was weary from hunger and tempted by the devil to turn stones to bread, replied, "It is written, 'One does not live by bread alone, but by every word that comes from the mouth of God'" (Matthew 4:4).

Daily prayer does not even have to involve a very large time commitment; some days we may spend just a few meaningful moments in prayer. On days when we have more time to devote to it, we may spend an hour or so in prayer and reflection. The important thing is to make a daily appointment for prayer and *keep this appointment.* A lapse of one day may lead to one lapse after another.

The book you are holding in your hands—*A Woman's Daily Prayer Book*—can be your guide in your prayer life. There is an entry for each day of the year, and each entry begins with a brief Bible passage. Each passage is followed by a reflection that opens up an aspect of the Bible passage for consideration as well as

conversation with God. A closing thought or quote supports each entry and brings a final bit of encouragement or insight to the topic at hand.

Whether you take out this book every morning as you sit back with your cup of coffee or tea, or whether you prefer to block out a bit of time during your lunch hour or before you go to bed, this book will help make prayer an easy habit. It will keep you on a prayerful path all year long.

While its content is inspiring, *A Woman's Daily Prayer Book* is also intended to be a beautiful feast for the senses. You will take pride in leaving it out in a place where you can see it and be reminded to take that bit of time every day to feed your soul.

A Woman's Daily Prayer Book is special because it addresses the specific prayer needs of women. Women have unique daily issues and challenges. How do we balance career, family, and "me time" with God's time? How do we balance our need to feel beautiful, valued, and useful while still giving due reverence and glory to God? How do we stay on the right side of despair when the house is a wreck, our children are struggling at school, and we are barely keeping up at work? All things are possible through prayer. Turn the page and make your prayer life a priority today!

January

January 1

For God did not give us a spirit of cowardice, but rather a spirit of power and of love and of self-discipline.

2 Timothy 1:7

Lord, I'm looking forward to this New Year. It is full of promise and hope, though I know that challenges will surely come as well. I know you have all the courage, strength, faithfulness, and love I need to meet each moment from a perspective of peace. I just need to stay tethered to you in prayer, listening for your Spirit to guide me and turn my thoughts continually back toward you. That's the key to a good day, a good year—a good life.

In the power of God's Spirit, every worthy goal is attainable.

January 2

I am about to do a new thing; now it springs forth,
do you not perceive it?

Isaiah 43:19

Lord, the best thing about the New Year is the word *new*! All the resolutions I make are meaningless unless I am truly new from the inside out. Give me a new attitude, Lord! A new focus,

a new passion, a new mission— all based on the new things you want to do through me this year.

No change endures unless it is accompanied by a change of heart.

January 3

No testing has overtaken you that is not common to everyone. God is faithful, and he will not let you be tested beyond your strength, but with the testing he will also provide the way out so that you may be able to endure it.

1 Corinthians 10:13

I am grateful that every temptation has an escape hatch, Lord. I want to be a woman who is in the habit of looking for the way out of a tempting circumstance, not lingering in the snare zone. No matter how powerful the lure might be, help me resist the bait. Keep reminding me that your ways are best. They are filled with peace and satisfaction, and they never leave a trace of regret lingering in my soul.

How to escape temptation:
Step one: Look for the escape route. (Pray!)
Step two: Take the escape route. (Run!)
Step three: Enjoy your freedom. (Dance!)

January 4

You have multiplied, O Lord my God, your wondrous deeds and your thoughts toward us; none can compare with you.

Psalm 40:5

Lord, help my eyes to see all the ways you are working in this world. Because of your great compassion, because of your active involvement, the

effects of everything you accomplish are multiplied many times over. We praise you, Lord, and pray you will continue to be involved in our lives and in our world. And may our deeds and thoughts always honor you.

Deeds and thoughts that honor God may go unnoticed on earth, but they are celebrated in heaven.

January 5

Every generous act of giving, with every perfect gift,
is from above, coming down from the Father of lights,
with whom there is no variation or shadow due to change.

James 1:17

The "season of giving" has just passed, but in your love, Lord, the gifts just keep flowing into my life moment by moment. The new day, the wonders of the season, all the things I take for granted, such as breathing, sipping a mug of hot tea, or enjoying a warm shower—each is a gift from your goodness. As I reflect on your generosity, I'm deeply appreciative for all you've given me.

The best kinds of gifts are simple and fulfilling.

January 6

O sing to the Lord a new song,
for he has done marvelous things.

Psalm 98:1

ord, this year I pray I will stop taking all your miraculous works for granted. Whether I praise you through song, words, or actions, I want to praise you not only for what you are doing, but also for all you have done in the past. Help me see the holiness of the ordinary in each day of this New Year.

Miracles are all around us; if we slow down and pay attention, we will spot them everywhere.

January 7

He knows the way that I take; when he has tested me, I shall come out like gold.

Job 23:10

think it's good for me to be able to see my frustrations, difficulties, and sorrows as "proving grounds" for my growing trust in you, Lord. From difficulty finding fulfilling work to bills I'm struggling to pay to a disagreement with a loved one, life brings every kind of opportunity for me to look to you for help. Today is a great day to choose to not get wrapped around my own axle when I'm faced with frustrations and fears. I'm putting all of the "proving ground" stuff I'm facing right now into your hands, and I trust you with the outcome.

Faith isn't magic; it's a choice to trust God, even when we are confused or sad.

January 8

I am the Lord, and there is no other;
besides me there is no god.

Isaiah 45:5

Lord, as I clean out closets and make lists for the New Year, show me any "gods" I have placed before you. Help me to look honestly at how I spend my time and my money. Does one of these areas of investment reveal a strong allegiance to something other than you? If so, Lord, help me eradicate those distractions from my life once and for all.

We put our souls in God's hands because we know that if God inspects them regularly, they will work as they should.

—Fulton Sheen

January 9

Keep alert, stand firm in your faith, be courageous,
be strong. Let all that you do be done in love.

1 Corinthians 16:13–14

The first part of this passage conjures images of a soldier decked out in full combat gear, and the second part makes me think of my grandmother. Trying to synthesize the two looks like my grandmother in camouflage and face paint with a tin of oatmeal cookies in her hand. The Christian life is kind of like that, though; we're called to be tough in our commitment to trusting God and yet tender-hearted toward all those around us. Combat boots and cookies—the life of a Christian in action. Lord, help me be strong in faith and gentle in love today.

A Christian won't allow her convictions to so carry her away that she would trample a soul to uphold a principle.

January 10

Happy are those who live in your house,
ever singing your praise.

Psalm 84:4

ord, today my heart is full of gratitude for your church. Thank you for asking us to meet together to honor you. What power there is in voicing our thanks and petitions together! What comfort in the outstretched arms of friends! Protect us, Lord. Keep us strong—now and in the days to come.

Church is the one place you can go just as you are and leave just as God sees you.

January 11

*Beloved, since God loved us so much,
we also ought to love one another.*

1 John 4:11

*F*ather, nothing moves me more to love others
than reflecting on how you love me. I think
of all the things you could have held against me and
used as reasons to not love me. And yet you always
look for ways to forgive, restore our relationship, and
move forward. I want to love like that!

*When I allow myself to be filled
with God's love, his love reaches out
through me to others in amazing ways.*

17

January 12

Whatever your hand finds to do, do with your might.

Ecclesiastes 9:10

Today I am tired, Lord. There seem to be too many things on my to-do list and too few hours in the day. And still, I know what a blessing it is to have work to do and to live a purpose-filled life. Thank you for tasks large and small that give meaning to our days, Lord. May we always do each one as if we were doing it only for you. And may we never assume we can do anything without your direction and energy.

The smallest task accomplished with the Lord has more impact than any material achievement.

January 13

*Therefore, I tell you, her sins, which were many,
have been forgiven; hence she has shown great love.
But the one to whom little is forgiven, loves little.*

Luke 7:47

Lord, it is tempting and easy to cast a scornful eye on those around us and note every fault. When my pride tempts me to do so, prompt me to turn the magnifying glass on myself instead. If I keep in mind how much I need your forgiveness every day, my love for you will never grow cold. I know you are willing to forgive each and every fault if I only ask.

*To handle yourself, use your head;
to handle others, use your heart.*

—Eleanor Roosevelt

January 14

*My father is glorified by this, that you
bear much fruit and become my disciples.*

John 15:8

ord, how I pray that your love is evident in
me today! I want to follow you closely and
help draw others to you as well. I know that if those
with whom I come in contact see love, joy, peace,
patience, kindness, goodness, faithfulness, gentleness,
and self-control in me, they may find you as well.
Direct my steps as I follow you, Lord, and may the
grace you've sprinkled on me be revealed for your
glory. Amen.

*If a disciple I would be,
the fruit of the Spirit must be seen in me!*

January 15

Do not store up for yourselves treasures on earth,
where moth and rust consume and where thieves
break in and steal; but store up for yourselves
treasures in heaven, where neither moth nor rust
consumes and where thieves do not break in and steal.
For where your treasure is, there your heart will be also.

Matthew 6:19–21

Okay, Lord, I know "it's only stuff," but much
of it is useful, and I want to take good
care of it. Help me see the
line between wanting to
be a good steward and
caring too much about
material things. That
line is often blurry from
my earthly perspective.
Help me be a responsible
caretaker without putting
too much value on mere
"stuff."

We are what we repeatedly do.

—Aristotle

January 16

Weeping may linger for the night,
but joy comes with the morning.

Psalm 30:5

ord, only you can comfort us when we grieve.
The heaviness we feel at such times can make
even breathing a struggle. But you, O Lord, stay close.
You fill us with your peace and your comfort. You
never let us retreat completely from your light into
the darkness of despair. And finally, in your time,
you restore joy to our souls. We are ever so grateful,
O Great Comforter.

Only God can turn heartache
into hope, despair into deliverance.

January 17

*I am the good shepherd. I know
my own and my own know me.*

John 10:14

Your Word
says—and I've
heard it elsewhere—
that a flock of sheep
knows its own
shepherd's voice and
won't respond to the
voice of a different
shepherd. It's true of
my relationship with
you, too, Lord: I *know*
your voice. I know when you're speaking to my heart,
and I know when I'm being coaxed by "other voices"—
wrong desires, worldly values, anxiety, pride, and the
like. Thanks for helping me see the difference. Coax me
to follow the sound of your voice today and always.

*The best leader always has
the best interests of his followers at heart.*

January 18

Trust in the Lord with all your heart,
and do not rely on your own insight.

Proverbs 3:5

Lord, how it must amuse you at times to see us orchestrating the details of our days as if everything and everyone were in our control. It's only when you are involved in our plans that things go smoothly, Lord. Teach us to trust that your way is

the better way, even when we can't see how every detail will turn out. Our insight is only as good as our reliance on you. Please be with us each day, Lord.

If you want to make
God laugh, tell him
your plans.
—Anonymous

January 19

Take care that you do not despise one of
these little ones; for, I tell you, in heaven their angels
continually see the face of my Father in heaven.

Matthew 18:10

I want to pray for the children in my life, Father. They're so innocent, and this world can sometimes be a harsh place. Thank you for assigning them a special place in your care and for giving their guardian angels direct access to you at all times. Be with them today, protect them—heart, soul, mind, and body. I know they will thrive in your love.

All night, all day,
Angels watching over me, my Lord.
All night, all day,
Angels watching over me.
Sun is a-setting in the west;
Angels watching over me, my Lord.
Sleep my child, take your rest;
Angels watching over me.

—African Spiritual

January 20

Even to your old age I am he,
even when you turn gray I will carry you.

Isaiah 46:4

Lord, today I ask your special blessing on the elderly among us. No matter how old we are, we notice our bodies aging. How difficult it must be to be near the end of life and struggling to hold on to mobility, vision, hearing, and wellness of being. Give us compassion for those older than

we are, Lord, and thank you for your promise that you will be with us to the very end of our days.

Those who trust in the Lord
may die with an aged body,
but they die young in spirit.

January 21

Those who oppress the poor insult their Maker,
but those who are kind to the needy honor him.

Proverbs 14:31

I long to help every needy person in the world, Lord. Perhaps the most effective way to do this is by praying that you will send help wherever it is needed. Meanwhile, there is my corner of the universe with its many needs, and some of these are surely within my reach: half of my sandwich to the person standing near the freeway ramp with a sign; an evening spent going through my closet and setting aside items to donate; a weekend afternoon of helping with events at my church; a monthly visit to the sick, homebound, or imprisoned. It's a privilege to honor you by extending your compassion—in person.

Keep the light on in your heart so that people alone in the dark can find their way home to God.

January 22

The earth is the Lord's and all that is in it,
the world, and those who live in it.

Psalm 24:1

Lord God, why is it that we tend to hold so tightly to the things of this world? We know in our hearts that everything we have is ours only by your grace and great generosity. When we accumulate more than we need, it only builds barriers between ourselves and you. Thank you for your provision, Lord. May we learn to hold everything loosely, knowing it is only borrowed.

We should not be concerned about
accumulating too little, but too much.

January 23

*By wisdom a house is built, and by understanding
it is established; by knowledge the rooms are filled with
all precious and pleasant riches.*

Proverbs 24:3–4

Thank you for your wise ways, Lord. Following
them fills my life with true blessings—the
riches of love and relationship, joy and provision,
peace and protection. I remember reading in your
Word that whenever I ask for your wisdom from a
faith-filled heart,
you will give it,
no holds barred.
So I'll ask once
again today for
your insight and
understanding as
I build, using your
blueprints.

*Whenever we try to "wing it" without
God's help, we end up "hoofing it"
through places we never intended to go.*

January 24

Commit your way to the Lord; trust in him, and he will act.

Psalm 37:5

ord, this is one of those days when I really
don't know which way to turn. I've lost my
sense of direction and feel as if I'm sitting on a rock in
the forest, wondering which trail will take me back to
familiar ground. Lead me, Lord. Send the signs I need
to follow to get where you want me to go. I put my
trust in you.

Like a modern-day GPS, God will
graciously redirect us once we ask for his help.

Our steps are made firm by the Lord, when he delights in our way; though we stumble, we shall not fall headlong, for the Lord holds us by the hand.

Psalm 37:23–24

tumbling happens. Don't I know it! I can get bummed out just by reviewing my mistakes and mess-ups from yesterday. But thankfully, I don't need to! God has hold of my hand. My worst

blunders—even if they've been truly harmful to myself or others—are not the end of the world. God will bring a new day, a fresh start, a redeemed relationship, a restored soul.

Though the toddler trips, the guardian grasps the little hand to lend the strength to stay upright. The adult's grip tightens, the grown-up muscles lift and hold, the child regains footing, and they continue on their way. God is always at the ready to lend us strength—all we have to do is ask.

January 26

*Call to me and I will answer you, and will tell you great
and hidden things that you have not known.*

Jeremiah 33:3

Lord, so often I keep doing the same things
over and over and getting the same
unsatisfying results. This is when I need for you to
shine your light on my life and reveal to me all that
I haven't been able to see through human eyes. You
have all knowledge and every answer to the mysteries
of heaven and earth. Show me, Lord. Give me just a
bit more of the knowledge you possess. Thank you.

*Listening to God is always the key
to revealing any mystery.*

January 27

For the Lord is good; his steadfast love endures forever,
and his faithfulness to all generations.

Psalm 100:5

Lord, if I were to boil down all the good news
in the universe and look to see what I'd
ended up with, there would be the eternal realities of
your goodness, your love,
and your faithfulness. And
in this world, I don't have
to look far for them—
family, food, shelter,
clothing, seasons, tides,
sun, moon, stars, life,
beauty, truth, salvation.
And that's just a sampling,
a preview of a much
longer list. I'm moved to
praise you and to tell you
how much I love you back.

While the rest of creation praises God just
by existing, humanity has the privilege of praising
him through premeditated word and deed.

January 28

*Even fools who keep silent are considered
wise; when they close their lips,
they are deemed intelligent.*

Proverbs 17:28

ord, I knew the minute the words were out of
my mouth that they would have been better
left unsaid. Why do I continue to fall into the trap of
needing to say what I think at the expense of someone
else? Not only did I hurt someone's feelings, but I also
looked like a fool in the process! Help me to repair the
damage and learn from
this experience. Give
me another chance to
behave nobly by saying
nothing.

*Lord, keep your arm
around my shoulders and
your hand over my mouth.*

—Anonymous

January 29

*Where can I go from your spirit? Or where can
I flee from your presence? If I ascend to heaven,
you are there; if I make my bed in Sheol, you are there.
If I take the wings of the morning and settle at the
farthest limits of the sea, even there your hand shall lead
me, and your right hand shall hold me fast.*

Psalm 139:7–10

The threat "You can run but you can't hide"
gets turned on its head in this passage—
transformed into a promise of God's presence with
us in all places. The Lord isn't ever going to be left
behind when we're in a place that seems distant or
unfamiliar. In fact, he's already there. It's a great truth
to keep in mind whether we're headed to the dentist
today or on a trip around the world.

*For those who trust in God,
the safest place in the world is
wherever he leads us.*

January 30

To him belong the glory and the power
forever and ever. Amen.

1 Peter 4:11

ord, we live in a world where there is a great
clamoring for power and glory. Greed runs
rampant, and time and again we see the inglorious
results of someone's unethical attempts to climb
to the top. Protect us from such fruitless ambition,
Lord. For we know that it is only when we humble
ourselves that you will lift us up higher than we could
ever have imagined. All power and glory is yours,
forever and ever. Until we acknowledge that truth, we
will never be great in anyone's eyes—especially yours.

Humility is the Christian's greatest honor; and the
higher men climb, the further they are from heaven.

—Jane Porter

January 31

We know that all things work together for good for those who love God, who are called according to his purpose.

Romans 8:28

Lord, this morning as I was folding a beautiful quilt a friend made for me, I thought again about how all the parts of our lives come together to form something beautiful and useful. Even the mistakes I would love to be able to erase from my memory helped

make me who I am today; I'm grateful I've been able to see the good that could come of them. May I always look back without regret and look forward with hope, knowing that when all is said and done my life will have been full—and wonderful.

I've been driven many times to my knees by the overwhelming conviction that I had nowhere else to go.

—Abraham Lincoln

February

February 1

The Lord is near to all who call on him,
to all who call on him in truth.

Psalm 145:18

Some people feel guilty for resorting to prayers of desperation. But God never turns away anyone who sincerely turns to him for help. Even when we've been distant, not walking close to him, he doesn't despise our cries for help as we look to get in step with him again.

It's a great relief to pray when you know how good God is and that his goodness isn't based on your own.

February 2

*When I look at your heavens, the work of
your fingers, the moon and the stars that you have
established; what are human beings that you are mindful
of them, mortals that you care for them?*

Psalm 8:3–4

ord, it's so easy for us to get bogged down
in the details of life on this earth. But when
we have the opportunity to gaze up at the stars on
a clear night, it is easy to remember that there is
so much more to your creation than our relatively
insignificant lives. You
placed the stars and know
them by name, Lord, and
you know us by name
too. We are blessed to be
even a tiny part of your
magnificent creation! That
you also care so deeply for
us is the best gift of all.

*Grateful will I always
be that he who hung
the stars made me!*

February 3

*Many waters cannot quench love, neither
can floods drown it. If one offered for love all the wealth
of his house, it would be utterly scorned.*

Song of Solomon 8:7

know yours is a persistent devotion, Lord.
Your devoted love for me is the example
that helps me to love others as well. What would I
prefer to your
love? What could
I love more than
those I hold dear?
Nothing in the
universe! Who are
the loves of my
life? Let me count
them all and
delight in them
today.

*Be sure the ones you love know
how much they mean to you.*

February 4

With the Lord one day is like a thousand years,
and a thousand years are like one day.

2 Peter 3:8

Keep us from being slaves to time, Lord. You always create time and space for anything we are doing that brings you glory. Teach us to rest in the knowledge that time is in your hands. Whenever we think we don't have enough of it, show us you have plenty and are happy to share! Thank you, Lord, for your generous supply of time.

You will never "find" time for anything.
If you want time you must make it.

—Charles Buxton

February 5

An open rebuke is better than hidden love! Wounds from a sincere friend are better than many kisses from an enemy.

Proverbs 27:5–6 NLT

Father, it stings when the ones I love correct me. I don't like to be wrong or feel like I'm being criticized. But that's just wounded pride revealing itself. Deep down I appreciate learning the truth so I can learn and grow. Flattery feels nice in the moment, but it doesn't do much real good. People who risk hurting me because they love me are the ones I should listen to. Help me get over my wounded pride quickly and move on in light of what I've learned.

And bless those who care enough for me to speak the truth in love.

It's great to love the truth, but it's greater still to speak the truth in love.

February 6

Blessed be his glorious name forever;
may his glory fill the whole earth.

Psalm 72:19

Lord, we praise you for all the beauty and
wonder you've placed in the world. How
creative of you to think of a creature as exuberant
and joyful as the hummingbird! How interesting that
you sprinkled spots on the backs of the newborn
fawns that follow along behind their mother through
our backyard. Let us never become so accustomed to
your glorious creation that we take it for granted,
Lord. You've blessed us with a wonderland, and we
thank you for it.

The world is God's
epistle to mankind—
his thoughts are
flashing upon us from
every direction.

—Plato

February 7

A gossip goes about telling secrets, but one who is trustworthy in spirit keeps a confidence.

Proverbs 11:13

From personal experience, I think "spilling the beans" sounds too harmless to describe gossip, Lord. I've had so-called "spilled beans" tarnish my reputation, harm relationships, and expose parts of my soul I wanted kept private. But the bright side is that I've learned the importance of finding trustworthy confidants—and of being one. Still, there are times when I'm tempted to talk when I shouldn't or am careless with my "thinking out loud." Help me guard the dignity of those who have confided in me by keeping quiet or speaking only when, how, and where I should.

If a confidence left in your care is restless to be let out, remember that it can never be retrieved once you open the gate.

February 8

Do not let loyalty and faithfulness forsake you; bind them around your neck, write them on the tablet of your heart.

Proverbs 3:3

Lord, how I long to stand strong in the faith! I read of the martyrs of old and question my own loyalty and courage. Would I, if my life depended on it, say, "Yes, I believe in God"? I pray I would, Lord. Continue to prepare me for any opportunity to stand firm for what I know to be true. To live with less conviction is hardly to live at all.

*Unless we stand up for the good,
nothing else we do will matter.*

February 9

*So acknowledge today and take to heart
that the Lord is God in heaven above and on
the earth beneath; there is no other.*

Deuteronomy 4:39

Lord, it is tempting to get entangled in the things of this world. When I get too caught up in the rat race or keeping up with the Joneses, prod me to step back, reflect, and call to mind what is truly important: Making time for conversation with you.

*Security is knowing that
God is in control,
and I am not.*

February 10

We are the clay, and you are our potter;
we are all the work of your hand.

Isaiah 64:8

ere we are again, Lord. Another time when I feel like I've made a complete mess of this life you've given me. I place myself in your hands. If you need to totally reshape me to turn me into someone more useful, so be it! Thank you for not abandoning me, your humble creation. Make me over in your design.

Only God can give us an extreme makeover from the inside out.

48

February 11

*Even youths will faint and be weary, and the
young will fall exhausted; but those who wait
for the Lord shall renew their strength, they shall
mount up with wings like eagles, they shall run and
not be weary, they shall walk and not faint.*

Isaiah 40:30–31

When I can't keep up with the younger set, I like to remember this verse, Lord. I may not have all the physical stamina and endurance I once had, but spiritually you have taught me what it means to tap into a strength far beyond my own—yours. I see it in the way you carry me through hardships and trials that at first seemed unbearable. I see it in the day-to-day "small things," such as prayer, that you've helped me to establish in my life. Wings of eagles, indeed! I'm soaring on your strength at this very moment.

*Spiritual flying lessons are simple:
Wait for and trust in God.*

February 12

We know love by this, that he laid down his life for us—and we ought to lay down our lives for one another.

1 John 3:16

acrifice doesn't always come easily, Lord. Please show me those opportunities you have placed in my day for me to lay down my own to-do list and be aware of the greater things you are doing through me. Don't let me miss those opportunities, Lord. Please do not allow any grumbling on my part to deter your work. Grant me the grace to make any sacrifices you need from me today.

Until we can lay it all down, nothing we pick up will be of any value to the world.

February 13

Blessed are those who mourn,
for they will be comforted.

Matthew 5:4

When sorrow comes to us, it can be overwhelming. We feel unable to move and incapable of the patience necessary to wait for the healing that will come with time. Knowing you are there, Lord, brings the most comfort.

It is even harder to watch a loved one grieve. We feel left outside with no way to reach in and bring comfort. Words fail. Kind gestures fall short. But when we remember that what comforts us most is your presence, we know what to do: just *be* there—listening, praying, and loving—allowing your Spirit to pervade the space around us.

The essence of comfort isn't in words; it's in one soul
bringing peace to another, without needing words.

February 14

*God is love, and those who abide in love abide
in God, and God abides in them.*

1 John 4:16

Lord, your gift of love is often distorted
in this world of ours. You are the source
of the only perfect love we will ever know. Thank you,
Lord, for abiding in us and helping us love ourselves
and others. On this day, Lord, I pray that you will
draw near to anyone who is feeling unloved. May they
accept your unconditional love so they will know what
true love is!

*God's love
dwells in us
and sustains
us. It never
disappoints.*

February 15

Do not worry, saying, "What will we eat?" or "What will we drink?" or "What will we wear?" . . . indeed your heavenly Father knows that you need all these things. But strive first for the kingdom of God and his righteousness, and all these things will be given to you as well.

Matthew 6:31–33

Prioritizing spiritual realities over temporal ones is not always easy. The physical realities are tangible. I can hold a stack of bills in my hand and know that if I don't pay them, problems will arise. But those spiritual realities . . . well, the benefits (and consequences) are not always so easy to recognize or see in the moment. This is a faith issue, pure and simple. First, I need to stay calm about issues of provision. Second, I need to keep drawing near to you. Third, I need to reach out to others with your love. And after all of these things are done, I need to trust you with the results.

Trust is easiest when its object is known to be trustworthy, and God has never once failed.

February 16

Turn my eyes from looking at vanities;
give me life in your ways.

Psalm 119:37

Lord, how
many
distractions there are
in this world! How
easy it is for us to get
caught up in the desire
to acquire, moving
from one purchase
to the next. How
tempting to read one
self-help book after another, until we are dizzy. Lord,
I know that true contentment, true beauty, and true
wisdom are all found only in your Word. Protect me
from focusing too much on material things.

February 17

But love your enemies... and you will be
children of the Most High; for he is kind
to the ungrateful and the wicked.
Be merciful, just as your Father is merciful.

Luke 6:35–36

This directive is so hard, Lord. I want to live as you ask, but sometimes I long to see those who've hurt me "get what's coming to them." I desperately need you to help me refocus. When I am mired in bitterness, Lord, prod me to meditate on the mercy you've freely given me—even when I have been most undeserving. Then, Father, grant me the grace to love those who have done me harm—not because they deserve it, but because they are precious to you.

The cross reminds us that the deepest love can carry the deepest pain.

February 18

My grace is sufficient for you,
for power is made perfect in weakness.

2 Corinthians 12:9

Lord, once again I am aware that you, by your grace, gave me the strength to work through a situation that I was woefully unprepared to face. I accept that when we are completely out of ideas, drained of all energy, and so sick at heart we can barely breathe, your grace and strength lift us up and carry us forward.
Thank you, Lord.

Remember, there is
a reason they call it
"amazing" grace!

February 19

But to all who received [Christ Jesus],
who believed in his name, he gave power to become
children of God, who were born, not of blood or of the will
of the flesh or of the will of man, but of God.

John 1:12–13

Spiritual birth is amazing, Father! It's a miracle no less exciting than the birth of a baby. Your Word says that it causes even the angels in heaven to rejoice. Thank you for my own spiritual birth. It's the reason I'm praying right now and enjoying this fellowship with you. It's so good to be your child. Today I'll just bask in that reality.

The privilege of belonging to God is greater than we can fully realize now, but we will eventually comprehend it in the light of eternity.

February 20

*I will turn the darkness before them into light,
the rough places into level ground.*

Isaiah 42:16

ord, how grateful I am that you are willing
to go before me to prepare the way. Even
when I sense that a new opportunity is from you and
has your blessing, I've learned I still need to stop and
ask you to lead before I take the first step. Otherwise
I will stumble along in the dark tripping over stones
of my own creation! Everything goes more smoothly
when you are involved, Lord.

*The path is always easier when
prayer paves the way!*

February 21

*Do all things without murmuring and arguing, so that you
may be blameless and innocent, children of God without
blemish in the midst of a crooked and perverse generation,
in which you shine like stars in the world.*

Philippians 2:14–15

ord, I admit that my light often shines more
brightly outside the walls of my home than
inside. The truth is that my family members—the ones
dearest to me in the world—are usually the first ones
to hear my murmuring and arguing and to see my
"blemishes." And to add insult to injury, they're often
the last ones to hear my confessions and apologies.
There are plenty of excuses I could make about
being around them more, having to deal with *their*
"blemishes," and about needing to "be me" at home.
I want to be consistent in my walk with you, though.
Give me the fortitude to shine my light *first* at home
and *then* into the world
around me.

*The kind of star I want to be
in this world has nothing to do
with Hollywood and everything
to do with heaven.*

February 22

From the end of the earth I call to you, when my heart is faint. Lead me to the rock that is higher than I; for you are my refuge, a strong tower against the enemy.

Psalm 61:2–3

ord, how we want to run to you in times of need—and how blessed we are that we always find you available. You always take us in and calm our weary spirits. You, O Lord, are mighty and unchangeable! At times when everything seems shaky and uncertain, you are firm and immovable. We praise you, Lord!

On Christ, the solid Rock, I stand:
All other ground is sinking sand.

—Edward Mote

February 23

Train yourself in godliness, for, while physical training is of some value, godliness is valuable in every way, holding promise for both the present life and the life to come.

1 Timothy 4:7–8

I know it is important to be physically healthy and strong, but how much the better if we're also spiritually strong! Sure, lifting weights does our bodies good, but regularly picking up a Bible is good for the health of our souls. And rather than just doing deep knee bends to increase our physical strength, we can also regularly "hit our knees" in prayer to strengthen our core spirits.

Lord, I want your priorities to be in place for my whole being—heart, soul, mind, and body. Then I'll be in good shape for the present time and eternity.

February 24

Rejoice in the Lord always; again I will say, Rejoice.

Philippians 4:4

Lord, you are the source of all joy! Regardless of how happy we may feel at any given time, we know happiness is fleeting. Happiness, so dependent on temporary circumstances, is fickle and unpredictable. But joy in you is forever!

And so we come to you today, Lord, rejoicing in all you were, all you are, and all you will ever be. Because of you, we rejoice!

Nothing can rob us of our joy when it's joy in the Lord we possess.

February 25

*As a prisoner for the Lord, then, I urge you
to live a life worthy of the calling you have received.
Be completely humble and gentle; be patient, bearing with
one another in love. Make every effort to keep the
unity of the Spirit through the bond of peace.*

Ephesians 4:1–3 NIV

Father, unity among your people is precious to you—and precious to us as well. We cannot achieve it without your assistance, though. Help us to keep petty disagreements from dividing us. Give us the grace to work through any disagreement with love and understanding.

*The recipe for unity isn't complicated, but it takes
commitment, perseverance, and love.*

February 26

I lift up my eyes to the hills—from where will my help come? My help comes from the Lord, who made heaven and earth.

Psalm 121:1–2

Lord, today I pray for all those who are in desperate need of help in order to survive: victims of earthquakes and tornadoes, the homeless, and the physically and emotionally destitute people of our world. Make yourself known to them, Lord. May they all see that their true help comes only from you! You who created them will not leave them without help, nor without hope.

The only lasting help is the help that comes from the Lord.

64

February 27

Now faith is the assurance of things hoped for,
the conviction of things not seen.

Hebrews 11:1

uman faith lives between two extremes,
Lord: It's neither completely blind nor
able to see everything. It has plenty of evidence when
it steps out and
trusts you, but
it takes each
step with a good
many questions
still unanswered.
It's really quite
an adventure,
this life of faith.

And Lord, I must confess that experiencing your
faithfulness over time makes it easier and easier to
trust you with the unknown in life. Thank you for
your unshakable devotion.

Faith is, by nature, purposeful and
persistent, hopeful and prayerful.

February 28

The world and its desire are passing away,
but those who do the will of God live forever.

1 John 2:17

ord, I've stood by too many deathbeds to ever doubt that the adage "you can't take it with you" is absolutely true. We come into this world with nothing, and we leave with nothing. So why is it so tempting to spend so much of our lifetimes striving for more money and possessions? We forget that all those things are fleeting, and  that the only people who are impressed by what we accumulate are those whose values are worldly. But you, O God, are eternal! Thank you for providing a way for us to be with you forever.

Our life is frittered away by detail...
Simplify, simplify.

—Henry David Thoreau

66

February 29

In his hand is the life of every living thing
and the breath of every human being.

Job 12:10

Lord, with each breath I take I am aware that it is you who breathed life into me. My next breath is as dependent on you as my last breath was. And I can confidently rest in the knowledge that it will be you and you alone who will determine when the last breath leaves my body and I go to be with you. Today, Lord, I thank you for the gift of life and for each breath I take.

Breathe on me,
Breath of God,
Fill me with life anew,
That I may love what
Thou dost love,
And do what
Thou wouldst do.
—Edwin Hatch

March

So I say to you, Ask, and it will be given you; search, and you will find; knock, and the door will be opened for you. For everyone who asks receives, and everyone who searches finds, and for everyone who knocks, the door will be opened.

Luke 11:9–10

Lord, I know you will show your goodness and faithfulness to me if I just diligently seek you. The problem isn't your willingness to give, but my tendency to try to do everything by myself rather than leaning on and trusting in you. This silly inclination brings me needless stress and wastes precious time. Today I endeavor to lay my needs and troubles at your feet the minute I begin to feel the least bit overwhelmed.

The words ask, search, *and* knock *start with the letters* A, S, *and* K, *which spell* ask. *We can use this little acrostic to remind us to just* ask!

69

March 2

Christ Jesus came into the world to save sinners, of whom I am the foremost.

1 Timothy 1:15

Lord, today a little white lie slipped out of my mouth to save me from a trying commitment. As soon as I felt your little tug on my conscience, I knew I had to come clean about it and repair my relationship with you and with my friend. I know that the lie wasn't small in your eyes, and it was a reminder to me that I am always vulnerable to sin. If I didn't feel your nudge to repair the situation as quickly as possible, I might have fallen into a complacency that would make me vulnerable to any number of more serious sins. I thank you for nudging me, Lord, and for forgiving me, yet again.

Even minor sin harms our relationship with God and others.

March 3

With joy you will draw water from the wells of salvation.

Isaiah 12:3

When grief fills my heart, Father, whether I'm feeling loss, shame, betrayal, or some other sorrow, I know it's temporary, even though at times it feels as though it will never go away. I know that your future for me is joy, and when it comes, I will not reject it. Strengthen me with your joy today, Father. I need it to lift up my soul.

Joy is much deeper than mere happiness. Happiness is like a brook that can dry up when the sun gets too hot. But joy is like a vast water system that flows directly from the Lord, an unfailing source.

March 4

As for me and my household, we will serve the Lord.

Joshua 24:15

Lord, what compassion you showered on your people when you grouped us into families! Thank you, Lord, for the homes we are privileged to enjoy. We are thankful for these sanctuaries for our children and grandchildren. May our homes and our families honor you, Lord, in all we say and do within them. Dwell with us, Lord. You are always welcome.

Christ is the head of this house; the unseen guest in every room.

—Anonymous

March 5

You shall love the Lord your God with all your heart, and with all your soul, and with all your might.

This directive sounds simple, but it is a deep spiritual truth. It is the first step toward a true relationship with God. Yet too often my love for God takes a backseat to my work and play. I don't want that to happen today. Father in heaven, please grant me the grace to love you fully.

The most gracious command of all, full of divine intention to bless us, is the command to love God with every fiber of our being. If we focus on loving God, we will be full of his love. Goodness and love will surround us, and they will flow from us as well.

March 6

*Here is the lamb of God who takes away
the sin of the world!*

John 1:29

Lord, the world just wasn't ready for your appearance by the Jordan. There you were, the King they so desired, yet they didn't know you. Let us welcome you into our world today as wholeheartedly as John the Baptist did when you appeared in the flesh! For you came to be our hope and our salvation. Humbly he came, but mightily he saved.

March 7

*Martha was distracted by her many tasks; so she ... asked,
"Lord, do you not care that my sister has left me to do all
the work by myself? Tell her then to help me."
But the Lord answered her, "Martha, Martha, you are
worried and distracted by many things; there is need of
only one thing. Mary has chosen the better part,
which will not be taken away from her."*

Luke 10:40–42

I have Martha days and I have Mary days, Lord. Some days lend themselves more to a worshipful response to you than others do. But Mary didn't let everyday tasks distract her from a golden opportunity to glean wisdom from you, Lord. Help me in my quest to carve out time every day to be attentive to your Spirit. My to-do list will always be there on the back burner.

*Thank you for including the Martha and Mary story in
your Word, Lord. Many of us are like Martha, and I am
grateful that you speak lovingly to us about our tendencies
as you teach us to surrender to your peaceful ways.*

March 8

For I am longing to see you so that I may share with you some spiritual gift to strengthen you—or rather so that we may be mutually encouraged by each other's faith, both yours and mine.

Romans 1:11–12

Almighty God, of all the things you've created, friendship must be among your favorites. What a joy it is for me to be with my girlfriends, Lord. What encouragement and affirmation I get from them—and what correction if it's needed! I cried when one of my dearest friends told me she was moving two states away, but you, O Lord, have kept us close in heart. That's the beauty of true friendship. It isn't just for here and now. It's forever.

A true friend is the gift of God, and He only who made hearts can unite them.

—Robert South

Let your adornment be the inner self with
the lasting beauty of a gentle and quiet spirit,
which is very precious in God's sight.

1 Peter 3:4

ord, sometimes I long to stand out. I notice others with shinier hair, amazing figures, and impeccable outfits, and I feel so plain. At these times, help me to remember that I should be at work cultivating the gentle and quiet spirit that is precious to you. This type of spirit may not call out, "Here I am!" but over the long run, it accomplishes much. I am doing what I can, and I leave the rest to you. I trust that you will bring all to fruition.

All people are equally
precious in God's eyes.

March 10

*Finally, beloved, whatever is true, whatever
is honorable, whatever is just, whatever is pure,
whatever is pleasing, whatever is commendable,
if there is any excellence and if there is anything
worthy of praise, think about these things.*

Philippians 4:8

Lord, in your infinite wisdom you knew we
would need instruction for life, and so you
placed in your Word the guidelines for
living a productive life that brings you
glory. Your Word nurtures us
body and soul and keeps
our minds focused on the
beautiful, positive aspects
of life. Thank you, Lord, for
not leaving us here without a
guidebook. We'd be lost without
your Word.

*The Bible is the only instruction
book needed for this life.*

March 11

*Ever since the creation of the world [God's] eternal power
and divine nature, invisible though they are, have been
understood and seen through the things he has made.*

Romans 1:20

What "speaks" to you in nature? The amazing
variety of birds coming and going at your
bird feeder? The petals on those wildflowers by your
mailbox? The smell of the air after a rainstorm? The
night sky? Maybe you simply wonder how those
weeds can find a way to thrive in the cracks of the
sidewalk. Whatever impresses us among the things
God has made, it's a part of his messaging system to
us, inviting us to search him out and find relationship
with him.

*Father, from time to time,
send me loving reminders of
who you are and how
intimately you care for me.*

March 12

*No distrust made him waver concerning the
promise of God, but he grew strong in his faith as
he gave glory to God, being fully convinced that God
was able to do what he had promised.*

Romans 4:20–21

ather God, when I'm tempted to give up on
a task or a ministry opportunity, it helps to
read about Abraham, Moses, Joseph, David, Job—all
those whose times of trial and perseverance are so
beautifully preserved for us through your
Word. Once we become attuned to
your plan for our lives, we can
continue on with the certainty that
you always complete what you
start. We can stand firmly on your
promises, confident that you will
give us the strength we need to keep going. Thank
you for the faith of the ages, Lord! It is also the faith
for today.

*Faith goes up the stairs that love has made and
looks out of the windows which hope has opened.*

—Charles Haddon Spurgeon

March 13

O Lord, my heart is not lifted up, my eyes are
not raised too high; I do not occupy myself with
things too great and too marvelous for me.
But I have calmed and quieted my soul.

Psalm 131:1–2

Lord, it's wearying trying to be on the cutting edge, working to "be somebody," scrambling to get to the top of the mountain first. Sometimes I need to pull away from the rat race and be quiet; to put away my goals, appointments, and lists and just be with you, Lord. I crave the peace of your presence, and I need to feel held by you. Please pick me up and let me lean against your heart, which I know is full of love for me and all the world.

We may be many things in this world, but by heaven's reckoning, we are still the little children of our gracious Heavenly Father.

March 14

But you, O Lord, are a shield around me,
my glory, and the one who lifts up my head.

Psalm 3:3

Lord, you know how all-encompassing grief can be. The weight we carry is physical as well as emotional, and even getting up in the morning can seem like an impossible, pointless act. Thank you, Lord, for bringing us comfort during such times. Eventually the day comes when we have the pleasant realization that we actually feel a little invigorated. We hold our heads a little higher as you help us find joy in our memories and peace in the knowledge that our loved one is safe by your side, looking down on us over your shoulder.

Hold no man
responsible for
what he says
in his grief.
—The Talmud

March 15

The Lord is good to those who wait for him,
to the soul that seeks him. It is good that one
should wait quietly for the salvation of the Lord.

Lamentations 3:25–26

Waiting? Waiting is not my forte, Father. As someone who has a hard time waiting for the microwave to heat my lunch, waiting for your answers to prayer is sometimes excruciating. But I've come to see that these waiting periods are usually good for me. I grow in discipline, and I discover the peace of your presence.

Today I'll trade in my usual fretting and fidgeting for the patience and peace of quiet trust in God.

March 16

My flesh and my heart may fail, but God
is the strength of my heart and my portion forever.

Psalm 73:26

ord, just when I was thinking I was too
pooped to get through the day, I heard
a praise song on the radio. It reminded me of the
unending supply
of energy and
strength that is
ours through faith
in you! Thanks
for getting me
through the day
today, Lord. I
would be so lost
without you.

God always knows
just what we need,
and just when we
need it.

March 17

For this reason a man will leave his father and mother and be joined to his wife, and the two will become one flesh.

Ephesians 5:31

Lord, how grateful I am to have found the love of my life. May I never take him for granted. May I focus on his strengths and be quick to forget any silly disagreement. Help me to be his encourager and his friend as well as his lover. Protect the bond between us, Lord. Keep it strong, healthy, and loving.

It's easy to halve the potato when there's love.

—Irish Proverb

March 18

Teach me to do your will, for you are my God.
Let your good spirit lead me on a level path.

Psalm 143:10

Lord, I know it is your will for us to forgive those who do us wrong, and I know that once we do, everything goes so much more smoothly in our lives. We forgive because you first forgave us, and I'm starting to understand that. Help me to forgive, Lord. Take away the hurt and betrayal, and leave only your peace.

The will of God will never take you where the grace of God cannot protect you.

—Anonymous

March 19

The Lord does not see as mortals see; they look on the outward appearance, but the Lord looks on the heart.

1 Samuel 16:7

This would be a great verse to hang over my bathroom mirror, Lord! As I work on my outward appearance each morning, help me to remember that my inner person needs attention too—especially since that's what you focus on. Your evaluation of my heart is far more important to me than any human opinion about my appearance or fashion sense.

While you are proclaiming peace with your lips, be careful to have it even more fully in your heart.
—Francis of Assisi

March 20

Let us know, let us press on to know the Lord; his
appearing is as sure as the dawn; he will come to us like
the showers, like the spring rains that water the earth.

Hosea 6:3

How certain the seasons are, Lord! How
faithfully you usher them in one
after the other, each in its assigned order. The spring
has come with its rains once again, just as I knew it
would. And spring's
arrival reminds me
that you—the faithful
creator—have promised
to dwell with those
who long to know you,
those who search for
you and look for your
return.

We never have to wonder if the Lord
will appear as he promised—only when.

March 21

*You are worthy, our Lord and God, to receive glory
and honor and power, for you created all things,
and by your will they existed and were created.*

Revelation 4:11

I can't make a blade of grass grow, Lord.
By contrast, you created this entire
universe and all it contains. If that doesn't inspire
worship in my soul, I can't imagine what will. But the
truth is that it *does* put me in awe of you; it *does* stir
my heart to join in the worship of heaven.

*God created all things, and we are
humbled and amazed at his magnificence.*

March 22

He makes me lie down in green pastures;
he leads me beside still waters; he restores my soul.
He leads me in right paths for his name's sake.

Psalm 23:2–3

ord, how grateful we are for the rest you
bring to even the most harried souls. The
young soldier on the battlefield knows that peace,
and so does the young mother with many mouths to
feed but too little money in her bank account. You are
the one who brings us to the place of restoration in
our hearts and minds, Lord. Thank you for being our
shepherd.

When you can't
sleep, don't count
the sheep; talk to
the shepherd.

—Anonymous

March 23

Have unity of spirit, sympathy, love for
one another, a tender heart, and a humble mind.
Do not repay evil for evil or abuse for abuse; but, on the
contrary, repay with a blessing. It is for this that you were
called—that you might inherit a blessing.

1 Peter 3:8–9

Lord, the last thing I want to say to the person who tailgates me in traffic is "Bless you." And I certainly don't want to pray for him or her to have a good day. Oh, but how graciously you've blessed my life, even though I've acted like a jerk on countless

occasions. So please help me to peel my focus off of how I'm being treated and redirect it toward how I've been treated by you. Then I'll be able to draw from your great reservoir of mercy and pay it forward in the form of a blessing instead of a curse.

To curse is human, but to bless is divine.

March 24

Set your minds on things that are above,
not on things that are on earth.

Colossians 3:2

ord, how easily we are drawn into the headlines on tabloids while we stand in line at the grocery store. How tempting it is to stop to hear the latest gossip, listening when we shouldn't and repeating things we don't even know are true. Distract us from such things, Lord. Help us to avoid getting too immersed in the things of this world, for we know that we are just passing through on our way to our true home with you.

How heavenly it is to exchange
daily drivel for divine daydreams!

March 25

O Most High, when I am afraid, I put my trust
in you. In God, whose word I praise, in God I trust;
I am not afraid; what can flesh do to me?

Psalm 56:2–4

Lord, I know that it was not David's sling that won the victory against Goliath—it was David's trust in you. While David's older brothers and the other troops cowered in the camp because of Goliath's threats and taunts, David ran out to meet the giant in your name, Lord. It was you who gave that shepherd boy success. Oh, Lord! I want to be like David. I don't want to cower in fear, but to run out in faith to do your will.

Courage is fear holding on
a minute longer.
—George S. Patton

March 26

Do not be grieved, for the joy of the Lord is your strength.

Nehemiah 8:10

ord, my heart aches for my friend, who is undergoing chemotherapy. How it saps her energy, Lord. Sometimes it seems the cure is more devastating than the disease. Stay close to her in this time of healing, Lord. Bring her comfort, and fill her with the knowledge that she can find hope in you. I know you will lend her the strength she needs to get through this trying time.

Nothing heals like the empowering strength we find in the Lord.

March 27

If we walk in the light as he himself is in
the light, we have fellowship with one another, and the
blood of Jesus his Son cleanses us from all sin.

1 John 1:7

ord, there's that joy-filled song "Walkin' on Sunshine" that comes to mind when I read this verse. And for me, the happiness of being in the light with you, the delight of walking with you, and the ongoing fellowship with my brothers and sisters in you— all this knowing that you've washed my sins away—

walkin' on sunshine is just what it feels like. Thank you for calling me into your light!

Keep your face to the sunshine
and you will not see the shadows.

—Helen Keller

March 28

You shall be like a watered garden,
like a spring of water, whose waters never fail.

Isaiah 58:11

Lord, how precious water is to us, and how parched and desperate we are when it's in short supply. How grateful we are that in you we have access to the living water that will never run dry! Keep us mindful of that refreshing supply today, Lord. Fill us up, for we are thirsty.

May we be the vessels through which God's living water is poured onto a dry and dusty world.

March 29

*Rejoice always, pray without ceasing,
give thanks in all circumstances; for this is
the will of God in Christ Jesus for you.*

1 Thessalonians 5:16–18

How can I rejoice when I'm having "one of those days," Father? How can I pray continually when I feel overwhelmed?

When I look to Jesus' example, I find the answers I seek. He didn't stay on his knees 24/7, but he did maintain an ongoing dialogue with you. He acknowledged that he would prefer to avoid his cross, but he willingly took it up because it was necessary. He focused on the joy to come later, in due time.

I too can give thanks for the good things in my life, even when bad things are bearing down on me. I can keep up a dialogue with you as I go about my day, and I can be joyful in a deep abiding sense, knowing that all is in your hands.

When we make joy, prayer, and giving thanks our habit, we are able to handle troubles with courage and grace.

March 30

And those who know your name put their trust in you,
for you, O Lord, have not forsaken those who seek you.

Psalm 9:10

Lord, maybe it's in the times we aren't sure that you are hearing our prayers that we learn to trust you the most. Eventually—in your time—we hear your answer. We know that you are still sovereign, and all our hopes and dreams are safe in your hands. Even when the answer to a prayer is "no," we are comforted by the knowledge that you care about us and respond to our concerns in a way that will ultimately be for our good.

What is the secret to
long-term security?
Trust in God.

March 31

*I am the resurrection and the life.
Those who believe in me, even though they die,
will live, and everyone who lives and believes in me
will never die. Do you believe this?*

John 11:25–26

Lord, I do believe!
And because of
my hope of life with you
in eternity, there is all the
more meaning for life today.
There's meaning in my
choices, my relationships,
my work, my play, my
worship. It all matters, it all
counts, and I live knowing
one day I'll stand in your
presence with great joy.

*Even though we can't imagine what life in
eternity will be like, we can be sure it will be
wonderful beyond our wildest dreams.*

April

April 1

*It is better to hear the rebuke of the wise
than to hear the song of fools.*

Ecclesiastes 7:5

I do sometimes prefer frivolity and flattery to growing in the light of some uncomfortable truth, Lord. You can see where I'm prone to skirting the issues I need to deal with, and you know when I'm indulging in foolishness when I could be having a meaningful interaction with someone who walks in the truth. I know it's okay to

have fun, but it's good for me to look in the mirror regularly as well. Grant me the grace to soak in the wisdom that will change me for the better.

*Change isn't easy, but staying on the
wrong path leads to unnecessary heartache.*

April 2

So if anyone is in Christ, there is a
new creation: everything old has passed away;
see, everything has become new!

2 Corinthians 5:17

ord, sometimes I think back to who I was
before I knew you, and I don't even recognize
myself. That's how great the change is when you
make us new creations! I'm so glad that the person
I was isn't nearly as important in your eyes as the
person you know I can be. I may have been younger
and fitter then, but
I was lost on this
worldly adventure.
Thank you, Lord, for
claiming me as your
own and making
everything new in
my life!

Let us do more than accept our salvation—
let us prove our values in our daily lives.

April 3

So God created humankind in his image, in the image of
God he created them; male and female he created them.

Genesis 1:27

Many women take joy in the fact that our gender was custom-built by God. Through God's providence, our role in the world is unique as well...and indispensable. We are called by our creator to nurture the hearts and souls of those around us. We are also made to be able to sense and detect—call it women's intuition—subtle, sometimes intangible, realities. We bring special wisdom and insight to finding solutions to the problems that plague our world.

Delight in being a woman. Love God, and love those
around you in your unique, special way.

April 4

I urge that supplications, prayers, intercessions, and thanksgivings be made for everyone, for kings and all who are in high positions, so that we may lead a quiet and peaceable life in all godliness and dignity.

1 Timothy 2:1–2

Whether we keep an actual prayer list, a list in our heads, or no list at all, it is good to keep others in our prayers. We have the privilege of being able to pray for our family members, and what a relief it is to be able to entrust them to God's care when we feel disheartened or overwhelmed. The above passage reminds us to pray also for "all who are in high positions," which could include anyone from world leaders to our boss. Jesus even told us to pray for our enemies! There isn't a soul on the face of the earth who doesn't need prayer, who doesn't need God's

intervention in their lives. And who knows? Perhaps someone is praying for you, too—right at this very moment.

Lord, please put on my heart and mind today the people who are most in need of prayer.

April 5

The Lord passed before [Moses], and proclaimed, "The Lord, the Lord, a God merciful and gracious, slow to anger, and abounding in steadfast love and faithfulness."

Exodus 34:6

Why do some see you as an angry God, eager to squash us when we sin? Could it be that you've been misrepresented by some who have claimed to represent you? Perhaps. But maybe at times I myself have clung to such wrong notions about you when others have offended me. I paint you with a human brush with such thoughts as, *If I were in God's shoes, dealing with that jerk, I'd let that person have it.* But when I gather myself, I realize you see each of us as the beautiful being you intended; our failings may bring you sadness, but not hatred. Your perfection is made up not only of absolute holiness, but also of deep mercy. And how I need that mercy every day!

Lord, you have revealed yourself to be merciful, gracious, patient, full of faithful love; I place my trust in you today.

April 6

And this is eternal life, that they may know you, the only true God, and Jesus Christ whom you have sent.

John 17:3

Lord, I know I encounter them every day: your loved ones who are—on their own strength—desperately trying to make some sense out of this life. Help me reach out to them. Give me the words to say and the gentle approach that will lead them to the knowledge of you and to the immense blessings you want to bestow on them.

Wherever I go and whoever I be,
let something of Jesus be seen in me.

April 7

Let us run with perseverance the race that is set before us, looking to Jesus the pioneer and perfecter of our faith, who for the sake of the joy that was set before him endured the cross, disregarding its shame, and has taken his seat at the right hand of the throne of God.

Hebrews 12:1–2

Some days the race feels like a sprint, Lord, and on other days, a marathon. I want to press on, but I need you to infuse my spirit with your strength and steadfastness. I want to run and finish well. Thank you for beginning the work of faith in my life and for promising  not to stop working until my faith is complete.

Earthly races are named for their distances— a 10K run, for example, is ten kilometers. Our race in the faith is a "HeavenK." Go the distance!

April 8

But he was wounded for our transgressions, crushed
for our iniquities; upon him was the punishment that
made us whole, and by his bruises we are healed.

Isaiah 53:5

ord, we stand in awe of your great sacrifice
for us. Your journey to the cross is the reason
we are free from the destruction of sin. It's why we
can be forgiven and be united with you throughout
eternity. No sacrifice is too great in response to your
love for us. Keep us ever mindful, Lord. Keep us ever
grateful.

*All roads for Christians lead
to the cross; where we bow
down and worship our Lord.*

April 9

But [the angel] said to [the women], "Do not be
alarmed; you are looking for Jesus of Nazareth,
who was crucified. He has been raised; he is not here.
Look, there is the place they laid him."

Mark 16:6

esus had promised his followers that he
would die, then rise again. Sometimes he
spoke in parables, though, and perhaps they thought
(or hoped) he was speaking metaphorically. But then
on that morning—that mind-blowing morning—when
Jesus exited his tomb in triumph over our nemesis
death, there was no doubt that he had meant what
he had said. "Look!" the angel exclaimed. In other
words, "See for yourself that it's true." Jesus has risen,
and he opened the way to eternal life for all who
trust in him.

But the pains that he endured, Alleluia!
Our salvation have procured, Alleluia!
Now above the sky he's king, Alleluia!
Where the angels ever sing. Alleluia!

—Charles Wesley

April 10

*So they left the tomb quickly with fear
and great joy, and ran to tell his disciples.*

Matthew 28:8

Lord, how beautiful indeed are the feet that bring good news! I can't read the account of the women who visited your empty tomb without my heart beating a bit faster. As terrifying as the events preceding that first Easter morning were, how quickly utter grief turned into complete joy! Fill me with that joy, Lord. May it emanate from me and spread to others.

*The best witness is simply following
Christ's magnificent example.*

April 11

Just as Christ was raised from the dead by the glory of the Father, so we too might walk in newness of life.

Romans 6:4

Lord, today my heart goes out to all those whose past mistakes weigh them down and make any vision they have of their future dreary at best. Oh, that they might know you and the saving grace you bring! Draw near to them today, Lord. Reveal yourself to them in a way that will reach them, and through your mercy and forgiveness, bestow upon them a new vision—a new hope.

Every day in the Lord is a new day full of everlasting promise.

April 12

*For we do not have a high priest who is unable to
empathize with our weaknesses, but we have one
who has been tempted in every way, just as we are—
yet he did not sin. Let us then approach God's
throne of grace with confidence, so that we may receive
mercy and find grace to help us in our time of need.*

Hebrews 4:15–16 NIV

Lord, sometimes I fall so low that I feel
ashamed and unworthy of being in your
presence. At these times, remind me that it is never
too late to throw myself at your feet and beg for
your forgiveness and mercy. You are all good and all
powerful, and your
love for us never
wavers. I can become
whole and joyful
again through you.

*God's door is always
open to his children.*

April 13

Therefore, since we are justified by faith, we have peace with God through our Lord Jesus Christ, through whom we have obtained access to this grace in which we stand.

Romans 5:1–2

Every day I blow it. Every day I need your grace, Lord. I am thankful that it isn't necessary to live a perfect life to have access to your grace. If that were the case, I'd be in big trouble. But instead of turning your back on me when I veer from your paths, you are always ready to welcome me with open arms. You simply call me to trust in your saving, relationship-restoring grace. That's where I'm standing right now—in that amazing grace of yours, asking you to forgive and restore me once again so I can resume good fellowship with you.

Relationship with God fills life with joy.

*All praise to God, the Father of our Lord Jesus Christ.
God is our merciful Father and the source of all comfort.
He comforts us in all our troubles so that we can comfort
others. When they are troubled, we will be able to give
them the same comfort God has given us.*

2 Corinthians 1:3–4 NLT

Lord, only you can take all the heartaches
and failures in our lives and turn them into
compassionate messages of hope for others. We care
for an aging parent who passes away, and so are
able to relate to the needs
of the elderly around us.
We go through a divorce,
and we can then give
genuine advice during
our interactions with
single mothers. Our pain
becomes others' gain,

Lord. Sometimes looking back over our shoulders
brings us hope for the opportunities that are surely
ahead of us. Thank you for second chances.

*Comfort isn't ours alone—it is to be
shared with those we encounter each day.*

April 15

Give liberally and be ungrudging when you do so,
for on this account the Lord your God will bless you
in all your work and in all that you undertake. Since there
will never cease to be some in need on the earth,
I therefore command you, "Open your hand to the poor
and needy neighbor in your land."

Deuteronomy 15:10–11

Will there always be poor people among us? Yes. God's Word says as much, but it's not in the context of hopelessness. It's in the context of a command for us to be generous. And it's a very beautiful picture, really, of the heart of God toward all humanity. Our tangible gifts to help the poor mirror God's spiritual gifts that keep flowing toward us to meet our needs. As our hands extend food, clothing, and shelter to those who lack it, God's hands extend grace, mercy, and forgiveness to give us all that our needy souls lack.

Spread your love
everywhere you go.
—Mother Teresa

April 16

God said, "This is the sign of the covenant that
I make between me and you and every living creature that
is with you, for all future generations: I have
set my bow in the clouds, and it shall be a sign of the
covenant between me and the earth."

Genesis 9:12–13

G od gave the rainbow as a sign of his promise
to never flood the entire earth again. The
colors that spread out in spectrum, as sunlight passes
through water droplets in the sky, speak of God's
faithfulness in keeping his promise to Noah and to
all the generations that have followed. Faithfulness
marks God's character. It is who he is, through and
through. Let every rainbow we see remind us of God's
faithful love, and let praise flow from our hearts to
the one who always keeps his promises.

Lord, thank you for rainbows
and all other reminders of your
faithful love to me. Open my
eyes to see each one today so
I can delight in your promises
and give you praise.

April 17

*Happy are those who find wisdom, and those
who get understanding, for her income is better than
silver, and her revenue better than gold.*

Proverbs 3:13–14

ord, you know how much time and effort
I put into surrounding myself with my
favorite things. Sometimes I wonder if it's always
worth it. Please help me sort out what's truly valuable
and what I can do without. One thing I know is worth
pursuing is the wisdom found in your Word. As I read
it and your Spirit helps me to comprehend it, I feel
rich indeed.

*Spending time in God's Word
doesn't always feel like it's
producing much effect, but
be assured it is sinking in.
Like a seed planted in spring,
it will bloom in due time and
bring you great joy.*

April 18

How weighty to me are your thoughts,
O God! How vast is the sum of them!

Psalm 139:17

ord, I want my thoughts to be like your
thoughts. I want to discern what you discern
and have the insight you have into all that happens
in the world. I know that can never really be, Lord,
but if I am open to your Spirit at all times, perhaps I
can construe your hopes now and then. May my mind
never be so cluttered that I fail to receive a message
you are trying to share with me, Lord.

The knowledge God shares
with us is the deepest knowledge of all.

April 19

You shall not covet your neighbor's house...
or anything that belongs to your neighbor.

Exodus 20:17

Father, you've shown me that coveting isn't always as straightforward as wishing I had someone else's house or car. The covetous corruption that creeps in can wear any number of disguises, such as begrudging the fact that someone has been blessed in some way that I haven't. It can be despising someone else's success or hoping for their failure so I won't feel left behind. The list goes on, but the essence is my discontent with my own lot in life as I compare myself with someone else. Set me free today to enjoy the blessings you've provided without spoiling them by pointless comparisons.

The fire you kindle
for your enemy often
burns you more than him.

—Chinese Proverb

119

April 20

Many proclaim themselves loyal, but who can find one worthy of trust?

Proverbs 20:6

Lord, it's hard to mend a friendship when trust has been broken. And yet when we open your Word, we see how you continued to love your people even when they abandoned you again and again! Give us that same ability to love and forgive in the face of broken trust, Lord. Heal our relationships as only you can.

A wise man will make haste to forgive, because he knows the true value of time, and will not suffer it to pass away in unnecessary pain.

—Samuel Johnson

April 21

*Of course, there is great gain in godliness combined
with contentment; for we brought nothing into the world,
so that we can take nothing out of it; but if we have food
and clothing, we will be content with these.*

1 Timothy 6:6–8

ontent with just food and clothing? Really,
Lord? I'm thankful that you provide for my
basic needs, but there's much, much more on my wish
list. This passage makes me realize how much I expect
in life. Sometimes I act like I'm entitled to certain
things: a well-paying job for little effort on my part,
minimal traffic on the way to said job, restaurant
lunches every day, seamless relationships with loved
ones. Help me to be thankful for the countless
blessings in my life and to always
be ready to help others rather than
focusing on adding to my own stores.
Please guide me, Lord. I'm ready to
answer your call to contentment.

*This magnificent butterfly finds a little heap of dirt and sits
still on it; but man will never on his heap of mud keep still.*

—Joseph Conrad

April 22

*He will dwell with them as their God . . . he will
wipe every tear from their eyes.*

Revelation 21:3–4

Lord, on days when everything seems to
go wrong, help me to remember that you
are always nearby to offer comfort. It is easy to get
overwhelmed and feel lost and alone in this world,
but deep down I
know that is never
the case. You are
always at the ready
to help—I just need
to remember to take
a moment to stop,
breathe, and pray.

*Trials strengthen us
and bring us
closer to God.*

April 23

Oh, the joys of those who trust in the Lord, who have no confidence in the proud or in those who worship idols.

Psalm 40:4 NLT

Lord, if only all the false gods that lure us were clearly labeled. We are introduced to worldly ambition, wealth, physical perfection, romance—any number of attractive enticements—and it isn't until we realize that the pursuit of them is using up way too much of our resources that we discover we have made these things our gods. Forgive us, Lord. Help us to keep even good things in balance and never to pursue anything with more fervor than we pursue our relationship with you.

What satisfies the body rarely satisfies the soul.

April 24

*For it is the God who said, "Let light shine out
of darkness," who has shone in our hearts to give
the light of the knowledge of the glory of God
in the face of Jesus Christ.*

2 Corinthians 4:6

Lord, your Word is so alive—so vibrant—that it almost seems illuminated when I am reading it. When I am troubled, opening the Bible is like turning on a comforting light in a dark, gloomy room. Thank you, Lord, for loving us so much that you gave us your wisdom to illuminate our lives.

The Bible is the perfect instruction manual for life.

Prepare your minds for action; discipline yourselves; set all your hope on the grace that Jesus Christ will bring you when he is revealed.

1 Peter 1:13

Father, your Word makes it clear to me that the life of faith is not passive. While we wait for you to answer prayer, grant wisdom, and open doors, we also keep our minds sharp and our hearts strengthened by reading and studying your Word, by meeting with you in prayer, and by finding encouragement among other believers. These are the disciplines our souls need to stay focused on ever-present hope.

Self-control is one of the traits of a life guided by God's Spirit. Ask God for the discipline you need as you seek to stay in shape spiritually; he has promised to give his Spirit to those who ask him.

April 26

For thus said the Lord God, the Holy One of Israel:
In returning and rest you shall be saved; in
quietness and in trust shall be your strength.

Isaiah 30:15

You, O Lord, are our refuge. When the days are too full and sleep is hard to come by, we simply need to escape to a quiet place and call on you. In your presence we find strength for our work and peace for our troubled minds. We are grateful for the comfort of your embrace, Lord.

There is no better place to be than safe in God's arms.

126

April 27

The prayer of the righteous is powerful and effective.

James 5:16

oes this mean I need to seek out a super saint when I need real prayer power? Rarely do I consider myself particularly righteous, but then I remember that your Word says that I've been *made* righteous in Christ. It's not my righteousness that I'm counting on, but his. He is working his righteousness into my life day by day, but it's always his—not mine. That is reassuring and exciting! So even *my* prayers, as I walk in Christ's righteousness, can be powerful and effective...right here and now!

We are righteous when we are focused on the good, holy, and true.

April 28

Do not let your hearts be troubled.
Believe in God, believe also in me.

John 14:1

Lord, today I want to praise you for giving me the faith to believe, for faith itself is a gift from you. I lift up to you today all those I know who are having trouble accepting your gift of salvation. Be patient with them, Lord. Reveal yourself to them in a way that will reach them, and draw them into relationship with you. Our lives are incomplete without you, Lord. Send your grace to those who are struggling.

A faith-filled heart is close to God's heart.

April 29

Those who are wise understand these things;
those who are discerning know them. For the ways
of the Lord are right, and the upright walk in them,
but transgressors stumble in them.

Hosea 14:9

I am here right now, Father, because I
do want to walk in your ways. I know
the key is staying connected to you because the ways
of the world are all
around me, always
imposing a different set
of values and a different
worldview. Give me a
wise and discerning
heart in all things today
so I can stay on track.

If distracted from God's ways today,
immediately take the following steps:

1. Come clean. (Admit your fault to God.)
2. Get clean. (Receive God's forgiveness.)
3. Keep clean. (Walk on in God's ways.)

April 30

*I am confident of this, that the one who
began a good work among you will bring it
to completion by the day of Jesus Christ.*

Philippians 1:6

Lord, what a comfort it is to know that
you are working to perfect us even on
days when we feel anything but perfect. One day all
creation will be perfected. How we look forward to
that day when our faith is fully realized, and we are
complete in you!

*Be patient with me.
God isn't finished with me yet.*

—Anonymous

May

May 1

Blessed are those who hunger and thirst
for righteousness, for they will be filled.

Matthew 5:6

ord, if my hunger and thirst for your
righteousness could be satisfied by ordering
from a spiritual drive-thru, I'd want to supersize my
order! I so want to be like Christ. I want to have his
courage and humility, his strength and gentleness. I
don't want substitutes—such as pride that looks like
courage or fear that looks like humility. I want the
real deal. Thank you for the promise that you will
satisfy this craving of mine, this deep soul hunger to
be and do all that is right, true, and good.

God blesses
any sincere
desire for his
ways.

May 2

The wise woman builds her house, but the foolish tears it down with her own hands.

Proverbs 14:1

Lord, why is it that frustration sometimes turns to despair and self-destruction? There are so many destructive forces in the world as it is, why do I sometimes make a bad situation worse because of my bitter or hopeless attitude? How often I wish I could take back thoughtless, hurtful words I have said to a loved one during the course of a trying day. How many times I wish I could have a "do over." But there are no "do overs" in real life. Help me to make amends and handle things better the next time I am challenged.

I have learned from experience that the greater part of our happiness or misery depends on our dispositions and not on our circumstances.

—Martha Washington

May 3

*Indeed, God did not send the Son into the
world to condemn the world, but in order that
the world might be saved through him.*

John 3:17

I love this verse. It reveals that Jesus, who will one day judge the world, didn't come to us in that role at his first coming. His chief desire was to save us from the consequences of our wrong choices and our rejection of God. He paid our debts with his life, and now he's waiting for us to do our part—to turn around and be reconciled to God before the final judgment. Wow! Who has that kind of mercy? Our loving God.

*He left His Father's throne above
So free, so infinite His grace;
Emptied Himself of all but love,
And bled for Adam's helpless race...
Amazing love! How can it be
That Thou, my God, shouldst die for me!*

—Charles Wesley

May 4

*I call upon the Lord, who is worthy to be praised,
and I am saved from my enemies.*

2 Samuel 22:4

Lord, so often we find ourselves asking you to save us from bad situations only to discover you quietly revealing to us that we are our own worst enemies! Teach us to break destructive habits and to stop polluting our minds with negative thoughts, Lord. Save us from our enemies, even when it means you have to step in and save us from ourselves!

Above all the grace and the gifts that Christ gives to his beloved is that of overcoming self.

—Francis of Assisi

*Peace I leave with you; my peace I give to you.
I do not give to you as the world gives. Do not let your
hearts be troubled, and do not let them be afraid.*

John 14:27

This verse leaves the question of my peace up to me. Will I *let* my heart be troubled today? Will I *allow* myself to be afraid? Jesus' peace is here for me. He gave it to those who follow him as an assurance of his abiding presence. Will I choose to give it its place in my soul when troublesome things are jumping out at me or nipping at my heels? God, you

have provided a great ocean of peace for my soul. These waters can "take me away" as no bath product can.

Take a dip in God's ocean of peace right now. Dive in, lay back, and let the waters of his love carry you along as you trust him with all that is troubling you.

May 6

And all of us, with unveiled faces, seeing the glory of
the Lord as though reflected in a mirror, are being
transformed into the same image from one degree of glory
to another; for this comes from the Lord, the Spirit.

2 Corinthians 3:18

Lord, how much time do we spend looking
into a mirror, and how often do we see you
there? We were made in your image, but rather than
focusing on that, we often focus on all the things
we'd like to change. When others look at us, do they
see our meager attempts to make our lips fuller and
our eyelashes longer, or do they see the light of your
love shining through our eyes? Teach us to focus less
on our own appearance and concentrate more on
presenting your face to those around us. It is you the
world needs, not us.

God's light overpowers
the deepest wrinkles.

May 7

*Those of steadfast mind you keep in peace—
in peace because they trust in you.*

Isaiah 26:3

There is a unique toy on the market that reminds me of a mini Humpty Dumpty without legs. It is called a Weeble. The promotional jingle for it is "Weebles wobble, but they don't fall down!" Sometimes I feel like a Weeble, Lord, wobbling around—not falling, just unsteady in my faith. I know that my spiritual growth is a process, but I often get impatient. Please help me become more steadfast in trusting you. A bit less wobble will bring a lot more peace.

*A steady gaze at the goal makes
for a steady gait on the path.*

138

May 8

Charm is deceitful, and beauty is vain,
but a woman who fears the Lord is to be praised.

Proverbs 31:30

ord, today I will be in the spotlight. I've been given an opportunity to be in front of a group, and I want to do a good job conveying my important message. Be with me, Lord; I know that I can accomplish very little without your help, but anything is possible with your guidance. Keep me focused not on myself, but on the insight I have to share.

Wisdom emanates
from a heart that
loves the Lord.

May 9

Be mindful of your mercy, O Lord, and of
your steadfast love, for they have been from of old.
Do not remember the sins of my youth or my
transgressions; according to your steadfast love
remember me, for your goodness' sake, O Lord!

Psalm 25:6–7

Lord, sometimes my past rises up to haunt me—or worse yet, to bite me. These are the real-world consequences of poor choices I've made. But even though I'm reminded of them because of the cause-and-effect nature of things, once I confess them to you and receive your forgiveness, they are erased from your record book. So even when I'm reminded of my old sins in one way or another, help me to quickly let go of any guilt or shame that rears its ugly head. While consequences may linger, your forgiveness is complete. Thank you for that eternal reality.

I've heard it said that when we confess our
sins to God, he casts them in the deepest sea
and puts up a "No Fishing" sign.

May 10

As a mother comforts her child, so I will comfort you.

Isaiah 66:13

Lord, you know a mother's heart. You know the panic in the middle of the night when the fever won't go down. You know the butterflies in the stomach when the school bus pulls up to the curb, and a little one heads off to kindergarten. Bless all mothers, Lord. Give them your wisdom and encouragement throughout their busy day, and when the day is over, give them peace and blessed rest.

The source of human love is the mother.

—African Proverb

May 11

Whoever walks with the wise becomes wise,
but the companion of fools suffers harm.

Proverbs 13:20

This proverb reminds me of the balance that is necessary in life, Lord. Often I am the one learning from the wisdom and experience of others, but help me to stand tall and be a leader when a situation warrants it. Help me to give a good example and to be mindful of the company I keep. I am not here to judge, but I do want to keep company with those who are using their time on this earth in constructive rather than wasteful ways. Help me to heed the advice of those with more life experience and—when called—to lead with a strong, gentle example.

Wherever you are, it is your friends who make your world.

—William James

May 12

Then the woman left her water jar and went
back to the city. She said to the people, "Come and see
a man who told me everything I have ever done!"

John 4:28–29

ord, what comfort I find in the knowledge that you know everything I've ever done. I know going over my sins with you is still necessary for my growth and development, but it helps to know I'll never have to hear you say, "I can't believe you did that!" You know my strengths and my weaknesses. You know my joy and my shame. And yet you still forgive me and have hope for me. Thank you, Lord, for caring enough to truly know me—and for loving me anyway.

The Lord knows each of us better than we know ourselves.

The heavens are telling the glory of God; and the firmament proclaims his handiwork. Day to day pours forth speech, and night to night declares knowledge. There is no speech, nor are there words; their voice is not heard; yet their voice goes out through all the earth, and their words to the end of the world.

Psalm 19:1–4

reation shouts to me, Lord, about how amazing you are. I see the wonder of your wisdom in everything from the solar system to how bodies of water feed into one another to the life cycles of all living creatures. Everywhere I turn there is something that makes me think about how creative and insightful you are. Thank you for this universe that speaks without words. I hear it loud and clear, and it tells me of your magnificence.

There's nothing like an hour or two of stargazing to regain perspective on the greatness and goodness of God.

May 14

Do not worry about anything, but in everything
by prayer and supplication with thanksgiving let your
requests be made known to God. And the peace of God,
which surpasses all understanding, will guard your
hearts and your minds in Christ Jesus.

Philippians 4:6–7

ord, even though I know worry is a useless
waste of time and energy, it snares me again
and again. Thank you for helping me notice early on
that I'm about to wallow in worry once more. As I
give this situation to you, Lord, I release my need to
worry about it as well. Instead, I look for the blessings
in the midst of all that's going on and thank you
wholeheartedly for them. I willingly trade my worry
for your peace.

Worry is a sure sign
that we have forgotten
to trust in God.

May 15

*Love is patient; love is kind; love is not envious or boastful
or arrogant or rude. It does not insist on its own way;
it is not irritable or resentful; it does not rejoice in
wrongdoing, but rejoices in the truth. It bears all things,
believes all things, hopes all things, endures all things.*

1 Corinthians 13:4–7

I wish this could be the dictionary definition of love, Father. It hits the nail right on the head. It's also a serious "gut check" for me. Am I living up to this standard of love in my relationships at home, at work, at church, and in my neighborhood? As I spend time in prayer  right now, show me where love is lacking in my attitudes, words, and actions. Then please fill me up again with your perfect love for those around me.

Never lose a chance of saying a kind word.
—William Makepeace Thackeray

146

May 16

For God alone my soul waits in silence; from him
comes my salvation. He alone is my rock and
my salvation, my fortress; I shall never be shaken.

Psalm 62:1–2

Lord, today I pray for all those who have
sought all the wrong kinds of protection.
It's so easy for us to become obsessed with protecting
our marriages, our children, and our well-being to the
extent that we are in danger of losing our peace of
mind. Remind us all, Lord, that when we are in your
hands, we are in the best of hands. You will never fail
us. You will never renege
on your promises. With
you, we stand strong and
have great hope.

A mighty fortress is our God,
a bulwark never failing.

—Martin Luther

So let us not grow weary in doing what is right,
for we will reap at harvest-time, if we do not give up.

Galatians 6:9

ather, I appreciate this encouraging reminder for me to keep chugging along the "high road." When I'm doing the right thing, it can feel like I'm going backward sometimes—especially when I see others taking not-so-ethical shortcuts and "getting ahead." I confess that when I get tired and frustrated, those shortcuts can look mighty tempting. But taking them would sabotage the good things that are ahead—the good harvest you have in mind for me to enjoy. It's not worth a temporary lapse of integrity for a bit of ill-gained ease to forfeit the fruits of good labor—labor I hope will always honor you.

It is never too late
to be what you
might have been.

—George Eliot

May 18

[Jesus] called the crowd with his disciples,
and said to them, "If any want to become my followers,
let them deny themselves and take up their cross and
follow me…. For what will it profit them to gain
the whole world and forfeit their life?"

Mark 8:34, 36

Jesus, your purposes are eternal ones, and they're generally the opposite of all earthbound here-and-now mind-set. This verse makes it clear to me that it takes a committed heart and soul to follow you. So where I have become dusty or rusty in my attentiveness in following you, please come with the breath of your Spirit to refresh me and get me moving in your ways again.

Perhaps the most challenging aspect of following Jesus is
not any single great act of faith or commitment, but the
daily choices we make to walk in his footsteps.

May 19

*And whatever you do, in word or deed, do everything
in the name of the Lord Jesus, giving thanks
to God the Father through him.*

Colossians 3:17

Looking at almost any product in the store, shoppers can find some kind of indication of where the item was manufactured: "Made in Taiwan" or "Product of Canada" or "Handcrafted in India" are just a few of the designations out there in consumer land. Some countries are known for high-quality materials and craftsmanship, while others are known for taking any shortcut to offer lower prices.

Similarly, whatever Christians say and do goes out into the world stamped with Jesus' name on it. What kind of a reputation will our contributions to his name build in our corner of the world today? We should make sure our works follow the example he set for us.

*Let us endeavor so to live that
when we come to die even the
undertaker will be sorry.*

—Mark Twain

May 20

The Lord is your keeper; the Lord is your
shade at your right hand. The sun shall not strike you
by day, nor the moon by night.

Psalm 121:5–6

ord, fear has reared its ugly head again and
is trying to take me far away from you. Hold
me close, Lord. Even though I have momentarily lost
my footing in this world, please do not let fear steal
the peace I find in you. Give me the strength to turn
away from fear and stand
tall in the knowledge that
I am never alone.

Fear knocked at the door.
Faith answered.
No one was there.

—Anonymous

May 21

And without faith it is impossible to please God,
for whoever would approach him must believe
that he exists and that he rewards those who seek him.

Hebrews 11:6

here is plenty of evidence for the existence
of God, but if we could absolutely prove it,
faith wouldn't be necessary. Even with all the evidence
of creation and the soul, God left room for us to be
free beings. Freedom is what brings such creativity,
invention, and interest to the world.

Understanding is the reward of faith.
So do not seek to understand in order to believe,
but believe so that you may understand.

—Augustine of Hippo

May 22

And what does the Lord require of you but to do justice, and to love kindness, and to walk humbly with your God?

Micah 6:8

Lord, we pray for all those in positions of leadership in our government. The pressures and influences on them are of a magnitude we can only imagine. Watch over them, Lord. Reach out to them with your grace, and instill in them your character, your priorities, and your vision for our country and our world.

You can't stay angry at someone for whom you pray.

God is not a human being, that he should lie, or a mortal, that he should change his mind. Has he promised, and will he not do it? Has he spoken, and will he not fulfill it?

Numbers 23:19

hen you say something, Lord God, it is as good as done. It may not take place in the timing that I'd imagine or wish, but you are true to your word without fail. So when you tell me not to be anxious—but rather to pray and you will give me your peace—I'll just do that. When you say that you forgive me when I confess my sin, I'll believe that. When you tell me that I'm your child and that you rejoice over

me, I'll take pleasure in that. Whatever you say, I'll not doubt it. Thank you for your great and precious promises and for your absolute trustworthiness.

God's word is guaranteed for time and eternity.

Do not judge, so that you may not be judged.
For with the judgment you make you will be judged, and
the measure you give will be the measure you get.
Why do you see the speck in your neighbor's eye,
but do not notice the log in your own eye?

Matthew 7:1–3

ord, my pride sometimes tempts me to judge others. From celebrity magazines to reality TV to social networking, it seems that very little in life is private anymore. This does not explain away some of the comments I find myself making, though. Throughout your Word you make it clear that your gift of salvation is available to everyone. Put this utmost in my mind when my pride tempts me to pass judgment on those around me.

God alone has the right to justify or condemn,
for he knows the disposition of soul of
every man, his strength, his tendencies and gifts.

—Abba Dorotheus

May 25

Then Job... fell on the ground and worshipped.
He said, "Naked I came from my mother's womb, and
naked shall I return there; the Lord gave, and the Lord
has taken away; blessed be the name of the Lord."

Job 1:20–21

ord, if my world were turned upside down in
a single day like Job's was—losing everything
I owned, and far worse, all of my children being killed
by a natural disaster—I doubt worship would be
my instinctive response. But here is Job, recognizing
himself as a mere man and praising you because you
are God. He trusts your wisdom that reaches above
and beyond his overwhelming tragedy. Somehow, he
is able to understand that the blessings you gave him
are not his to hold on to or his that he can demand
repayment from you. Even Job's punishing trials could
not shake his faith
in you.

Oh, build in me
a faith that cannot
be lost in the
storms of life, Lord!

May 26

*This also comes from the Lord of hosts; he is
wonderful in counsel, and excellent in wisdom.*

Isaiah 28:29

ord, I looked at a recent problem from
every angle imaginable, but it wasn't
until I filtered it through your Word that the gems
of wisdom and understanding appeared. How lost
we would be without your guidance, Lord, and how
blessed we are to have your counsel.

*Hidden treasures of God's truth
are just waiting to be discovered.*

May 27

Even though I walk through the darkest valley,
I fear no evil; for you are with me.

Psalm 23:4

Within the valleys of mountainous terrain, darkness lingers long in the morning and swoops down to settle swiftly in the evening. The taller the surrounding mountaintops, the deeper and darker the valley. The psalm writer has one of these deep valleys in mind—a place where the path is shadowy and a chill is always in the air.

Yet here, in what some might call a godforsaken place, the psalm writer surprises us with these words: "I fear no evil; for you are with me." He surprises

and comforts us with his reminder that when we follow the Lord our shepherd, there is no such thing as a godforsaken place.

If I could choose anyone to be with me in my suffering, in my loneliness, in my sorrow, wouldn't the best choice be the one who discerns all and cares most about me?

Bear one another's burdens, and in this way
you will fulfill the law of Christ.

Galatians 6:2

Lord, I know my friend is overwhelmed right now. Just as you lift my burdens when I come to you in prayer, show me what I can do to make her load lighter. I lay her troubles before you, Lord. I know our efforts can lift her burdens.

For what are men better than sheep or goats
That nourish a blind life within the brain,
If, knowing God, they lift not hands of prayer
Both for themselves and those who call them friend?

—Alfred, Lord Tennyson

May 29

*The Lord is good, a stronghold in a
day of trouble; he protects those who take
refuge in him, even in a rushing flood.*

Nahum 1:7–8

Thank you, Lord, for the fact that when
difficulties and trouble start to accumulate
like waters at flood stage, I can find the high ground
of safety and security in you. I trust you today—trust
your goodness as
well as your promises
of protection and
care for me. And even
if everything I own
is swept away in the
flood, you will still
be there with me.
Remind me that the

stuff of this world is temporary, but my life in you is
kept safe both now and for eternity.

God enters by a private door into each individual.

—Ralph Waldo Emerson

Above all, maintain constant love for one another,
for love covers a multitude of sins.

1 Peter 4:8

ord, I know that all of your commandments
are important. I also know, though, that
you once said your greatest commandment, after
loving you, is for us to love one another. I think love
is so important because so many other good things
flow from love. If we love those around us, we will
never do anything to hurt them. If you see our loving
hearts in action, you can overlook and forgive any
number of our more minor failures.

Jesus, Thou art all
compassion,
Pure, unbounded
love Thou art;
Visit us with Thy
salvation,
Enter ev'ry
trembling heart.
—Charles Wesley

May 31

If you abide in me, and my words abide in you, ask for whatever you wish, and it will be done for you.

John 15:7

Lord, I deeply desire to abide in you. I desire to have you abiding in me as well, so closely that I can speak to you any time and feel your presence. Destroy the distractions that create distance between us, Lord. Clear out the clutter that keeps me from sensing your best plan for my life. Then when I ask for what I wish, it will be the fulfillment of your desire for me as well.

We know the truth, not only by the reason, but also by the heart.

—Blaise Pascal

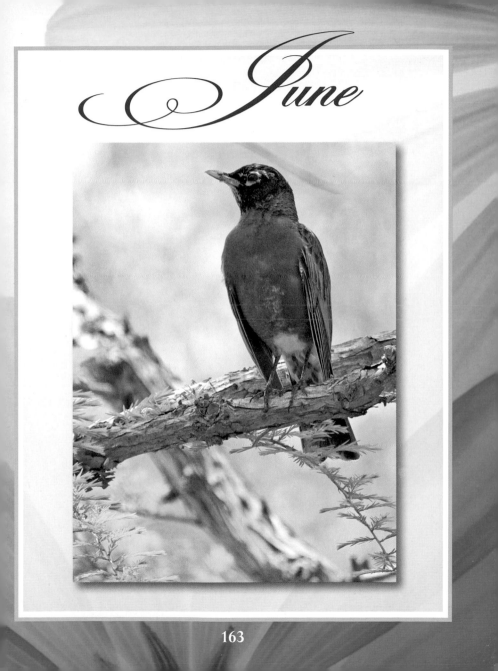

June

June 1

When he saw the crowds, he had compassion
for them, because they were harassed and helpless,
like sheep without a shepherd.

Matthew 9:36

ord, give me your compassion today. When
I look at the people around me, help me
to see them through your eyes. I know you love us
all equally, Lord. And you love us completely and
unconditionally. May I compassionately reach out to
others in your name today.

God loves each of us as if there were only one of us.

—Augustine of Hippo

June 2

And why do you worry about clothing?
Consider the lilies of the field, how they grow; they neither
toil nor spin, yet I tell you, even Solomon in all his glory
was not clothed like one of these.

Matthew 6:28–29

Lord, how freeing it is to rid our drawers and closets of unneeded clothing and pass it along to someone who can really use it! Thanks for reminding us that since you provide for our needs, we don't need to hold on to any surplus. Keep us mindful that true beauty comes not from the latest fashions but from hearts dedicated to sharing your love with the world.

The glory of the Lord is wondrously beautiful to behold!

June 3

*God is spirit, and those who worship him
must worship in spirit and truth.*

John 4:24

One phrase that has popped up in the Christian music market recently is "extreme worship." It seems that everything in our culture is moving toward some kind of extreme version of itself. We have extreme sports, extreme home improvement shows...and now extreme worship. But what God is looking for is not found in our form—it's found in the essence of our worship. It's not something anyone can readily identify by the *appearance* of a worshipper—it's something only God can see when he looks in our hearts.

*To worship well, don't worry about how you're doing;
think about all God is doing (and has done) in your life.
This way, the worship part will come naturally.*

June 4

Immediately the father of the child cried out,
"I believe; help my unbelief!"

Mark 9:24

ord, I know that doubts and confusion don't come from you. On days when everything I know to be true is challenged—and I feel like I'm walking through a fog that won't lift—be my source of truth and light. Bring me back to complete trust in you.

When you get into a tight place and everything goes against you till it seems as if you couldn't hold on a minute longer, never give up then, for that's just the place and time that the tide'll turn.

—Harriet Beecher Stowe

167

June 5

Yours, O Lord, are the greatness, the power,
the glory, the victory, and the majesty; for all that is
in the heavens and on the earth is yours.

1 Chronicles 29:11

Almighty God, do we tell you often enough how awesome you are? We stand before you in complete awe of your creation, your sovereignty, and your power. Let us never minimize the ability you have to change our reality

in an instant, even when it involves moving mountains or calming storms. You, O God, are the one and only God, and we give you glory at all times.

If God is willing to
move your mountain,
don't tell him
where to put it.

June 6

Be strong and courageous; do not be
frightened or dismayed, for the Lord your God
is with you wherever you go.

Joshua 1:9

ord, what a relief it is to know that
whether I'm going to the corner grocery
for milk and eggs or on a multicity adventure via
planes, trains, and automobiles, you are with me. You
never have a scheduling conflict, and you are more

necessary than my
car keys or boarding
pass. Thanks for
always coming
along, Lord. Some
days I could hardly
take a step outside
my house without
leaning on you.

This day be bread and peace my lot:
All else beneath the sun
Thou know'st if best bestow'd or not,
And let thy will be done.

—Alexander Pope

June 7

*I will greatly rejoice in the Lord, my whole being
shall exult in my God; for he has clothed me
with the garments of salvation, he has covered me
with the robe of righteousness, . . . as a bride
adorns herself with her jewels.*

Isaiah 61:10

hese are fantastic word pictures! Salvation
worn like a garment, righteousness donned
like a robe, and belonging to you revealed as a bride's
glittering accessories—that's how you describe my life
in you. And yet, I don't quite see it that way right
now. Please give me hope to believe this reality.

*Trust God's perspective. He sees the joy that lies ahead
when we are finally and fully united with him.*

June 8

For this slight momentary affliction is preparing us
for an eternal weight of glory beyond all measure,
because we look not at what can be seen
but at what cannot be seen; for what can be seen
is temporary, but what cannot be seen is eternal.

2 Corinthians 4:17–18

How can any affliction be considered slight? But then, it was the Apostle Paul, not some armchair life coach, who wrote these words. Paul was whipped, beaten, and almost killed by rock-throwing antagonists. At several times the victim of shipwrecks, Paul was exposed to the elements, then imprisoned and abandoned by friends who couldn't take the heat. But because Paul believed his future in Christ would hold great wonder and blessings, his passing hardships were of little consequence to him. He had his eyes on the prize, and in light of his goal, everything he had to go through to reach it was worth it.

All, everything that I
understand, I understand
only because I love.

—Leo Tolstoy

June 9

Oh, look on us, we pray,
for we are all your people.

Isaiah 64:9 NIV

Here we are again, Lord. Another time when I feel like I've made a complete mess of this life you've given me. I place myself in your hands. If you need to totally reshape me to turn me into someone more useful, so be it! Thank you for not abandoning me, your humble creation. Make me over in your design.

Only God can give us an extreme makeover from the inside out.

June 10

For all who are led by the Spirit of God
are children of God.

Romans 8:14

One sentiment I hear from time to time is "…after all, we're all God's children." It's usually uttered during trying times, to remind us to hold on and keep the faith. It's a comforting thought, but the verse here stresses that God's children are led by his Spirit. May we strive each day to be active children of God, praying and following the call of his Spirit rather than our own impulses and desires.

The measure of a man's real character is what he would
do if he knew he would never be found out.

—T. B. Macaulay

June 11

I pray that you may have the power to comprehend, with all the saints, what is the breadth and length and height and depth, and to know the love of Christ that surpasses knowledge, so that you may be filled with all the fullness of God.

Ephesians 3:18–19

Lord Jesus, the dimensions of your love are hard for me to comprehend because there is no other love like yours. No human love can compare with how deeply and thoroughly you love me. But just trusting that there is such a love as yours is the perfect beginning point for an adventure of becoming delightfully lost in its immensity.

Oh, the deep, deep love of Jesus,
Vast unmeasured, boundless free;
Rolling as a mighty ocean
In its fullness over me.
Underneath me, all around me,
Is the current of Thy love;
Leading onward, leading homeward,
To my glorious rest above.

—Samuel T. Francis

June 12

For where two or three are gathered in my name,
I am there among them.

Matthew 18:20

Lord, how comforting it is to know that you don't require large numbers of people to come together in order for you to be present. So often it's in the spontaneous coming together of two individuals who turn their hearts toward you that your presence is felt most clearly. Thank you for taking time to meet with us, Lord. May you always feel welcome.

God works and we work.
—Monastic Saying

175

June 13

He will guard the feet of his faithful ones,
but the wicked shall be cut off in darkness;
for not by might does one prevail.

1 Samuel 2:9

Every day I'm exposed to a world whose values don't jibe with yours, Lord. I am in need of constant reminders to not get caught up in notions that money, power, status, and physical appearance are of utmost importance. While the movers and shakers of society endorse such things as necessary for a fulfilling existence, you say that faithfulness to you is where real life is lived out and lasting inner peace is achieved. O Lord, help me when I'm tempted to believe that I can prevail in life by being seen as "strong" in ways that ultimately don't matter to you.

A man wrapped up in himself makes a very small bundle.

—Benjamin Franklin

June 14

*Devote yourselves to prayer, keeping alert
in it with thanksgiving.*

Colossians 4:2

Lord, if all the prayers ever prayed were
linked together, surely they would reach
to heaven and back countless times! We want to be a
people who pray without ceasing, Lord. Hear both the
prayers we utter and the silent prayers of our hearts,
and may you also sense how grateful we are to serve
a God who listens to our prayers and sends us his
answers.

*Prayer is not monologue, but dialogue; God's voice in
response to mine is its most essential part.*

—Andrew Murray

June 15

A person's pride will bring humiliation,
but one who is [humble] will obtain honor.

Proverbs 29:23

Someone may ask, "What's the difference between humility and humiliation?" A simple way to look at it is that humility is voluntary and peaceful, while humiliation is compulsory and painful. Practically speaking, it's better for me to think rightly about myself in relation to God and others (i.e., to walk in humility) than to think I'm "all that" and experience the humiliation of  an extreme reality check. As I walk in true humility, there's the added bonus that God will send honor my way—and the honor he will set up for me will be sweeter than any I could try to grab for myself.

Lord, please show me my blind spots of pride
so I can choose the path of humility now
and avoid the pain of humiliation later.

June 16

All things came into being through him,
and without him not one thing came into being.

John 1:3

ord, forgive us for those times we struggle
with an issue for longer than necessary
because we foolishly think it isn't worth your time.
We know that everything that exists, everything that
lives and breathes, everything that happens does so
with your full knowledge. Give us hearts and minds
that are open to this amazing truth.

Take comfort
and recollect
however little you
and I may know,
God knows . . . and
His mercy is over
all His works.
—Charles Kingsley

June 17

"Truly I tell you, whoever does not receive the kingdom of God as a little child will never enter it." And he took [the children] up in his arms, laid his hands on them, and blessed them.

Mark 10:15–16

Lord, sometimes when I speak to others about my faith, I see doubt in their faces. Faith in you doesn't always appeal to the "rational" adult in us, unfortunately. Please give us the grace that will enable us to come to you with open minds, open hearts—and open arms. I know that once we clear our minds of all that we think we know, all will become clear to us through you.

Being childlike isn't the same as being childish. Childishness would point to a lack of maturity, a lack of self-control, and a tendency toward foolishness. Childlikeness has to do with being innocent, humble, and full of love and awe.

June 18

Ascribe to the Lord the glory due his name;
bring an offering, and come before him.

1 Chronicles 16:29

ord, no matter what we bring of ourselves
to give you, even if we include all our
hopes and dreams, it's never enough to give in return
for all you've given to us. And so we give you our
praise. We sing to you and come before you with our
meager offerings, praying all the while that you will
make something marvelous of them.

God's gifts put man's best dreams to shame.

—Elizabeth Barrett Browning

June 19

*I have no greater joy than this, to hear that
my children are walking in the truth.*

3 John 1:4

ruth is a narrow road, and it's easy to
fall to one side or the other. For every
beautiful kernel of truth, there are a thousand lies
that can be made around it. Staying on the straight-
and-narrow would be impossible if it weren't for the
Spirit of God, who leads us to all truth. Delving into
God's Word with the
Holy Spirit to guide us is
the best way to stay on
track and keep walking
in the truth.

*It is a great thing to know
the season for speech and
the season for silence.*

—Seneca

June 20

*Blessed are those who have not seen
and yet have come to believe.*

John 20:29

Lord, how blessed we are to be able to see
you all around us and to sense your presence
within us. Even though we can't see you in the same
way we might see a friend or a neighbor, we see you
in your Word and in all that is good and true in the
world around us. Thank you, Lord, for making yourself
so available to us.

*All I have seen teaches me to trust
the Creator for all I have not seen.*

—Ralph Waldo Emerson

June 21

If any of you is lacking in wisdom, ask God, who gives to all generously and ungrudgingly, and it will be given you.

James 1:5

Well, Lord, since you're offering, I'm not going to be shy about asking. I need wisdom. I need it today as I'm dealing with people and situations and wondering what the best approach or decision might be. Thank you for being generous with your gifts rather than giving them to only a select few. In fact, you make receiving them as simple as just asking. You never cease to amaze me with your generosity, Lord. I'm deeply grateful.

No doubt allowed: The only condition on this wisdom is that it be received with faith.

June 22

*In your hand are power and might; and it is in your hand
to make great and to give strength to all.*

1 Chronicles 29:12

Lord, today I pray for all struggling parents.
Give them strength to hold fast to what they
know is right even in the face of conflicting opinions
and advice that is well meaning but off the mark
nonetheless. You alone can supply the peace of mind
they need to get through the toughest of times. Stay
close to them, Lord, and amaze them with your works!

*We are all prodigals
in the process of
returning home
to the Father.*

June 23

But the wisdom from above is first pure, then peaceable, gentle, willing to yield, full of mercy and good fruits, without a trace of partiality or hypocrisy.

James 3:17

When I read this verse, I realize how perfectly Jesus personified heavenly wisdom. It's a wonder to me that we are called to walk in his footsteps, but then I remember that it is only possible to do it through the Spirit that works in and through us. Thank you, Lord, for making the things of heaven available to those who seek them.

Wisdom doesn't look like an old guy who sits on the mountaintop while pilgrims make their way up to him for a word of advice. Wisdom looks like Jesus, who came down from heaven to meet us at our greatest point of need to minister God's grace and truth to us.

June 24

*Now may the Lord of peace himself give you
peace at all times in all ways.*

2 Thessalonians 3:16

Lord, you who brought peace in the midst
of the storm are the only one who can
bring peace to our world today. How much anger
we see raging around us, Lord. And the conflicts are
not limited
to wars on
foreign soil.
Rather they
rage in the
hearts and
minds of
many of us.
Be the source

of peace in every gathering storm, Lord. You are the
Prince of Peace, and we need you desperately.

As on the Sea of Galilee the Christ is whispering, "Peace."

—John Greenleaf Whittier

June 25

Let us test and examine our ways, and return to the Lord. Let us lift up our hearts as well as our hands to God in heaven.

Lamentations 3:40–41

The idea of an exam can strike fear into even the most prepared individuals. But the exam to which God's Word calls us is different from any dreaded math final or set of philosophical questions. This test is a self-checkup to see how we're doing—a chance to ask ourselves some probing questions and to answer them honestly. In the process,  if we give ourselves some not-so-good marks, we don't need to beat ourselves up or become discouraged. Instead, we can use what we learn to initiate a fresh starting point for getting back into fellowship with our Lord.

Lord, help me as I take inventory of my ways right now. Show me any junk I've acquired that needs to go so I can travel lighter, freer, and happier in you.

June 26

Be strong, and let your heart take courage,
all you who wait for the Lord.

Psalm 31:24

Lord, please forgive us in our impatient moments and nudge us back onto the right path. We live in a society that knows nothing of delayed gratification; we often get caught up in the expectation that everything we need from you and ask of you will happen immediately. But we know from cxpcricncc that your timing is always pcrfcct, Lord. We are blessed and privileged to have time for reflection and growth.

The Lord may not come when you call, but He is always on time.
—Anonymous

June 27

Now to him who is able to keep you from falling, and to make you stand without blemish in the presence of his glory with rejoicing, to the only God our Savior, through Jesus Christ our Lord, be glory, majesty, power, and authority, before all time and now and forever. Amen.

Jude 24–25

ord, I just want to tell you how much I love you, how grateful I am that you have taken me into your care. Ever since I've entrusted myself to you, you've kept me from becoming entangled in the kinds of things that would bring me to ruin. You fill

my heart and mind with peace as I stay close to you. It's a miracle of your grace that I am standing tall today, lifting my praise to you from a heart full of love.

In the depth of winter I finally learned that within me there lay an invincible summer.

—Albert Camus

June 28

Let us hold fast to the confession of our hope without
wavering, for he who has promised is faithful.

Hebrews 10:23

lmighty God, I know you are supremely
faithful! Today I ask you to restore hope
to the hopeless. Plant seeds of hope in hearts that
have lain fallow for so long. Send down showers of
hope on those struggling with illness, persecution,
or difficult relationships. Hope that comes from you
is hope with the power to sustain us when nothing
around us seems the least bit hopeful.

Knowing the source of all hope,
may we never be found hopeless.

June 29

And let us consider how to provoke one another to love and good deeds, not neglecting to meet together, as is the habit of some, but encouraging one another, and all the more as you see the Day approaching.

Hebrews 10:24–25

Many people commonly object to churchgoing, saying, "I don't need to go to church to be near God." It's true: One can be close to God without attending service. In fact, on the other side of the coin, some folks who go to church regularly live very "worldly" lives.

So what good is church? Church is good for God, for us, and for those around us. Gathering together reminds us of our need for God and satisfies God's need of a place in our harried lives. In addition, sometimes it is good for us to be there because others are in need of our presence and support. Simply put, church is not always about *our* needs. It is also about what God needs and what our neighbors need. Church creates a place for all of these needs to be met.

"Church life" doesn't happen only within the four walls of a steeple-topped building. It happens as we connect regularly with those around us.

192

June 30

*And remember, I am with you always,
to the end of the age.*

Matthew 28:20

ord, how humbly we acknowledge that we
are your disciples in this world—following
you and attempting to bring others to you as well.
We can't do it without you, Lord. But knowing that
you are always with us, we can be bold in any
situation. As we come to you and abide with you
again and again, we are filled with your Spirit. Then
we are prepared to be
your ambassadors in this
world.

*There are two ways of
spreading light—to be the
candle or the mirror
that reflects it.*
—Edith Wharton

July

July 1

Show yourself in all respects a model of good works.

Titus 2:7

Lord, thank you for calling me to yourself and then giving me your Spirit to strengthen me—heart, soul, mind, and body—to work in ways that bring honor to you. This goal of being a model of good works in every respect makes me realize how much I need you each moment. And as I grow in a life of doing what is right and true and good, help me grow in humility as well, remembering that you are the source of my strength.

God invites his children to work alongside him, learning to emulate his goodness.

July 2

In the morning, while it was still very dark, he got up and went out to a deserted place, and there he prayed.

Mark 1:35

Lord, how many times have I resolved to spend time first thing each morning in your Word and in prayer—and how many times have I neglected to do so! A day that begins with you, Lord, is sure to be a day blessed by you. Give me an insatiable thirst for time with you, Lord. And thank you for always being available to meet with me.

Rather than being so quick to think we're too busy to pray, we need to be quick to remind ourselves that we're too busy not to pray!

July 3

Indeed, the word of God is living and active,
sharper than any two-edged sword, piercing until it
divides soul from spirit, joints from marrow; it is able
to judge the thoughts and intentions of the heart.

Hebrews 4:12

Your Word really does cut to the heart of the matter when it comes to what life is about, Lord. It doesn't let me hide behind excuses, pretenses, or lies. It gives me the straight scoop without any meaningless frills. That kind of honesty is hard to find in this world—especially accompanied by the absolute love that fuels it. As you lay open my heart with your truth, help me not to run and hide; help me to trust your love enough to allow you to complete the "surgery" that will bring the health and well-being my soul longs for.

Love and truth are
inseparable in God's
character. He cannot love
without bringing truth,
and he never brings truth
without his love.

July 4

*Now the Lord is the Spirit, and where
the Spirit of the Lord is, there is freedom.*

2 Corinthians 3:17

Lord, how blessed we are to live in a country where we are free to worship as we please. Help us to never take such freedom for granted. Today we ask you to bless any believers who are being persecuted for living out their faith. Draw especially near to them, Lord. Surround them with your mighty army of angels.

*Long may our land be bright
with freedom's holy light;
protect us by Thy might,
Great God, our King!*

—Samuel F. Smith

July 5

Great and amazing are your deeds, Lord God the Almighty!
Just and true are your ways, King of the nations!

Revelation 15:3

*Y*ou are ultimately the one who permits nations and rulers to rise and fall, Lord. You alone are the King of Kings, and you do all things well—with righteousness, justice, and truth. When all is said and done, you won't allow evil to prevail. Indeed, all people—whether powerful or peasant, rich or poor—will be called to give you an account of how they've lived. In light of that, help me to live well today, honoring you in all I do.

In the eyes of God, the infinite spirit, all the millions that have lived and now live do not make a crowd. He only sees each individual.

—Søren Kierkegaard

July 6

For the promise is for you, for your children,
and for all who are far away, everyone whom the
Lord our God calls to him.

Acts 2:39

ord, how we
cling to your
promise that the Holy
Spirit is always near to all
who believe in you. How
comforting it is for us as
parents to know that our
children have the Holy
Spirit to guide them and
lead them into a purposeful
life. We praise you, Lord, for
your loving care for us and
for our children and grandchildren.

O Lord, I am afraid.—Take hold on me:
I am stronger than the sea.—
Save, Lord, I perish.—I have hold of thee.
I made and rule the sea,
I bring thee to the haven where thou wouldst be.

—Christina Rossetti

200

July 7

*For you were called to freedom, brothers
and sisters; only do not use your freedom as
an opportunity for self-indulgence.*

Galatians 5:13

love the freedoms I enjoy as your
child, Father. I also deeply appreciate
the freedoms I enjoy as a citizen of a free country.
Both citizenships—my heavenly one and my earthly
one—call for responsible living on my part, but these
responsibilities are really a joy and a privilege. Help
me to always keep this in the forefront of my mind as
I make choices each day.

*Freedom does require a bit of self-denial on our part, but
it's that very self-denial that frees us from the tyranny of
self-indulgence and makes us fit for free living.*

July 8

*For through him both of us have access in
one Spirit to the Father.*

Ephesians 2:18

Lord, just as the Jews and Gentiles were all
presented the path leading to you, so are
all those in the world today. Search our hearts, Lord.
Don't let petty disagreements and differences of
opinion lead us astray. We are so lost without you,
Lord. Thank you for your open invitation to us all.

*As we get to know our neighbors, we realize
more things unite us than divide us.*

July 9

*And [Abram] believed the Lord; and the Lord
reckoned it to him as righteousness.*

Genesis 15:6

oday I'll simply trust you, Father. I'll
remember that you're not looking for
résumés full of impressive credentials; rather, you seek
hearts that trust in you. You want to enjoy a vibrant,
meaningful relationship with me—a relationship in
which I trust you fully. That's the starting point of a
life lived for you.

*Love, trust, and respect are
foundational in any good
relationship, including my
relationship with God.*

203

July 10

Now that you have purified your souls by your obedience to the truth so that you have genuine mutual love, love one another deeply from the heart.

1 Peter 1:22

Lord, you are so serious about our loving one another that you even ask us to love our enemies. You are not satisfied if we merely pretend to love them either—you want us to genuinely love them! Such love demands more of us than we have to give, Lord. Only by drawing on the powerful love you offer will we be able to

love all those around us. Stay with us always, Lord, and sustain our love for each other.

Looking back, I have this to regret, that too often when I loved, I did not say so.

—David Grayson

July 11

Hannah prayed and said, "My heart exults in the Lord; my strength is exalted in my God.... I rejoice in my victory.

1 Samuel 2:1

Victories—both big and small—are sweet when they come from you, God. Promotions, honors, breakthroughs, discoveries, answered prayers... it's fun to savor them and know that your gracious hand has provided them. Help me remember to thank you when I taste victory today and to give you praise in all circumstances. My greatest reward in this life is your abiding presence with me.

There are no losers in the kingdom of God. Christ has secured victory for us over sin and death by his own death and resurrection. We are forever winners in him!

July 12

And this is the boldness we have in him, that if we ask anything according to his will, he hears us.

1 John 5:14

Lord, thank you for always listening to my concerns. So often I begin praying in one direction only to sense you turning my thoughts around until I end up praying for something quite different. Only later do I realize you were gently guiding me in a better direction. What blessed communication! I am so grateful.

The Lord not only hears but also values our prayers, especially when we are humble and sincere.

206

July 13

For who is God, but the Lord? And who is a rock,
except our God? The God who has girded me with
strength has opened wide my path. He made my feet like
the feet of deer, and set me secure on the heights.

2 Samuel 22:32–34

Trying to tackle life without God is like making your way alone through a dense jungle filled with all sorts of perils. It is rough going—discouraging, disheartening, and often disastrous. On the other hand, the life of faith is one of being led on a well-kept path. Even though trouble may come along, it cannot overwhelm us because the Lord strengthens and guards our souls when we call on him for help.

Father, I entrust my soul to your care today.
No matter what may be around the next bend
in the road, I know you will lead me safely through it.

July 14

Two are better than one, because they have a good reward for their toil. For if they fall, one will lift up the other.

Ecclesiastes 4:9–10

Lord, so many times when I've been down, time with a good friend has lifted me up again and helped me to face my circumstances with a better attitude. Sometimes that friend is my best friend—my husband—but other times it's one of my precious female friends who seems to intuitively know the precise advice I need. Thank you, Lord, for dear friends. May I be such a friend to others.

Those who are the hardest to love, need it the most.

—Socrates

July 15

*But you will receive power when the Holy Spirit
has come upon you; and you will be my witnesses
in Jerusalem, in all Judea and Samaria,
and to the ends of the earth.*

Acts 1:8

ord, as
I walk
in your spirit of
strength and love
today, may others
see what life in
you is like. It isn't
mere religion or a
list of rules and regulations. Rather, it's real life full
of adventure, challenge, wonder, joy, and peace—all in
the context of relationship with you as I live through
the energy you provide. Thank you for the spirit
of boldness that enables me to live out my faith
without fear.

*A life of prayer keeps us plugged into our power source,
ensures our tank of love is filled up, and puts the wind in
our sails to follow through on our commitments.*

July 16

I do not consider that I have made it my own; but this one thing I do: forgetting what lies behind and straining forward to what lies ahead, I press on toward the goal for the prize of the heavenly call of God in Christ Jesus.

Philippians 3:13–14

ord, what good does it do to dwell on past mistakes? You tell us to look forward, not back, and yet we play failures and sins over and over in our minds. We know those thoughts aren't from you, Lord. Keep our minds focused on the truth of your salvation and on the new life we have in you.

We don't put photos of our failures in our scrapbooks, so why store them in our minds?

July 17

Draw near to God, and he will draw near to you.

James 4:8

I remember hearing someone say once, "If God seems far away, guess who moved?" It's true, Lord: Sometimes I drift far away from you. I neglect reading your Word, I let my prayer life go by the wayside, and I get all tangled up in my attempts to handle everything on my own. I usually come to a sudden realization of how much I need you, and I am grateful for the epiphany! Even though I'm the one who's moved so far away, you don't hold it against me; you simply call me back.

When we take even the littlest step toward God, he closes the gap between us with one giant step toward us.

July 18

I am not asking you to take them out of the world,
but I ask you to protect them from the evil one.

John 17:15

Lord, how unworthy we feel of your son's prayers on our behalf, but how grateful we are for his intercession! It's all more marvelous, more mysterious than we can grasp, but because we trust your Word and your heart, we humbly thank him for caring so much about us. Surely his prayers are heard above all others!

As Jesus prayed for us, so we must pray for one another.

July 19

The law of the Lord is perfect, reviving the soul; the decrees of the Lord are sure, making wise the simple; the precepts of the Lord are right, rejoicing the heart.... More to be desired are they than gold, even much fine gold; sweeter also than honey, and drippings of the honeycomb.

Psalm 19:7–8, 10

Lord, do I value your word more than I value my paycheck? Do I crave it and savor it like I do chocolate? Do I roll it over in my mind, pondering how insightful, how wise, how wonderful your thoughts, works, and ways are? Train my heart and mind to love your Word—to grasp all the depths of it and hold it close to my heart as the great treasure that it is.

It is only in recent history that the Bible has been made accessible to so many. We have it in our own language, often with multiple copies on hand— something people in times past would have cherished, something for which we should be grateful.

July 20

*In everything do to others as you
would have them do to you.*

Matthew 7:12

ord, today I pray for your grace and mercy
to help me to live unselfishly. Putting others
first does not come naturally to me, Lord, but with
your help, I will stop and think before I speak or
act. I'm not at all confident in my ability to do that
without you, but I also know that anything is possible
when you are involved. Thank you, Lord.

What wisdom can you find that is greater than kindness?

—Jean-Jacques Rousseau

July 21

O Lord, our Sovereign, how majestic is your name in all the earth! You have set your glory above the heavens.

Psalm 8:1

This morning I am marveling at the birds at the bird feeder, Lord. Those little creatures are so fascinating! Their plumage, the variety of sizes, shapes, beaks, tails, wings, calls…I feel a sense of pure delight at their existence. I can find so many things to be in awe of in this great, wide universe you have made. You have made it all to speak of your majesty—to tell us what you are like. I turn my heart toward heaven today, to worship and give glory to you, Lord.

Pause to take in some element of the natural world today. Wait a few minutes while the wonder of it works on your soul, turns your heart toward God, and gives birth to a prayer.

July 22

I have called you friends, because I have made known to you everything that I have heard from my Father.

John 15:15

Lord, I am thankful every day that you sent your Son to live among us. How blessed we are that he taught us about you and gave us such a beautiful example to follow. May I remember every day to pause and give thanks for this, so I do not get too caught up in my trivial, worldly cares.

What a friend we have in Jesus,
all our sins and griefs to bear!

—Joseph M. Scriven

July 23

*Now may our Lord Jesus Christ himself and God
our Father, who loved us and through grace gave us
eternal comfort and good hope, comfort your hearts and
strengthen them in every good work and word.*

2 Thessalonians 2:16–17

Sometimes the circumstances of our lives
are so difficult, Lord! Often misfortunes
seem to come all at once. Other times ongoing, wear-
me-down situations or relationships seem to follow
us day in and day out. Then there are the crushing
tragedies that strike us in our tracks and devastate us.
A life of faith is not defined by these things—but it is
not exempt, either. Suffering is as real for the faithful
as for anyone else. However, we have an "eternal
comfort and good hope" that lifts us up. In
that comfort and hope, God carries us, heals
us with the balm of his tender mercies, and
strengthens us to carry on in what is good.

*Regardless of circumstances today,
may you keep the faith within the hope and
comfort of Christ's eternal love for you.*

July 24

Remember his covenant forever, the word that he commanded, for a thousand generations.

1 Chronicles 16:15

Almighty God, our faith in you is undergirded by your faithfulness. No matter how many times we turn away, you patiently wait for us to return to you. Instill in us that same sense of honor and faithfulness that is yours, Lord. May we be as faithful to you as you have been to us.

God always was, is now, and always will be faithful.

July 25

If the anger of the ruler rises against you, do not leave your post, for calmness will undo great offenses.

Ecclesiastes 10:4

ost of us know all too well what that moment is like—the panic that sets in when we realize we've made a major mistake at work. When we fall out of good graces with the person in charge, life can be very stressful. Such times tempt us to scramble to make amends or to just give up, defeated. The passage above is a great tip from the top. It was written by the most powerful king ever to rule in Israel. King Solomon *was* the ruler, and here he offers some insight about dealing with such an experience. The king's advice? Don't panic. Be calm. Listen well. Speak with a matter-of-fact, honest spirit. Solomon tells us that such a response will go a long way toward making amends.

Bravery is being the only person who knows you're afraid.

—Franklin P. Jones

July 26

Come to me, all you that are weary and
are carrying heavy burdens, and I will give you rest.

Matthew 11:28

Lord, I know you take notice of them—the caretakers for the aged and the ill. They work selflessly for the most vulnerable among us, yet their efforts are so often overlooked. May they sense your presence beside them, Lord. May they feel your strength lifting them up and helping them through the most trying moments. Give them encouragement by helping them see what a difference they make in their patients' lives.

God aids the valiant... both to you and me
He will give the help needed.

—Teresa of Avila

July 27

Blessed are the merciful,
for they will receive mercy.

Matthew 5:7

ercy is a beautiful word, Father. I breathe a sigh of relief just thinking about your mercy toward me. Help me to remember that—as the recipient of such generous forgiveness—I should be quick to forgive others, whether I am the victim of a minor thoughtless slight or some bigger affront.

We forgive to the extent that we love.

—François de La Rochefoucauld

July 28

I pray that the sharing of your faith may become effective when you perceive all the good that we may do for Christ.

Philemon 6

Lord, sometimes I am overwhelmed when I see all the suffering in this world. I feel like I am flailing in a treacherous sea with no power to be of any assistance to anyone else. Through prayer I regain my senses, and I know it's not up to me to meet all the needs in the world. Please show me which assignments belong to me; help me to focus on those and trust that you are working on the others.

Precisely this—not to be conscious of oneself as spirit—is despair, which is spiritlessness.

—Søren Kierkegaard

July 29

Though the fig tree does not blossom, and no fruit is on the vines; though the produce of the olive fails and the fields yield no food; though the flock is cut off from the fold and there is no herd in the stalls, yet I will rejoice in the Lord; I will exult in the God of my salvation.

Habakkuk 3:17–18

A modern-day equivalent of this verse might go something like this: Even though the world seems to be in turmoil and I am concerned for the future, still I will praise God each day because I know he is the source of my rescue. He protects me, provides for me, and knows what I need at every moment. Even on the darkest days he is nearby, loving me and sending me strength.

Still round the corner there may wait,
A new road or a secret gate.

—J.R.R. Tolkien

July 30

He said to me, . . . "Not by might, nor by power,
but by my spirit, says the Lord of hosts."

Zechariah 4:6

Lord, thank you for being a part of my work today. I can always tell when a thought or an idea comes from you because it's just too perfect to have been my own! That you care enough to be involved in my work is a precious gift to me, Lord— one I would never want to be without.

Our work is most productive when we partner with the Lord.

July 31

You are the light of the world.... [L]et your light shine before others, so that they may see your good works and give glory to your Father in heaven.

Matthew 5:14, 16

Jesus, you said these words to your followers, and they echo down through the centuries to meet me here, as I turn my heart toward you in prayer. As I think of the people you've brought into my life, I think of the times and ways your light has shined brightly through me. I'm also aware of things I do and say, as well as the attitudes I have, that dim or obscure that light at times. Please trim the wick of my words, today; clean the glass chimney of my attitudes; and add the fuel of good behavior to this lamp that is my life in you. I ask these things for the sake of your reputation and to the glory of your Father.

It takes only one lamp in a dark place to demonstrate the beauty and benefit of light.

August

August 1

The steadfast love of the Lord never ceases,
his mercies never come to an end; they are new every
morning; great is your faithfulness.

Lamentations 3:22–23

Feelings of love tend to ebb and flow, Lord, and too often my actions are the result of my overly sensitive nature. Thank you for your love, which flows like a steady stream. Thank you for mercies that never dry up, as seasonal brooks do. Help my love to be more like yours today. Keep me from selfishly withholding or retracting it when I'm hurt, angry, or disappointed. Let love flow more—not less—where it seems most undeserved. Help me conquer the troubles around me by means of a flood of merciful love.

Mercy is not easy to give, but it carries us into a place of great freedom and power—freedom from bitterness and anger, and power to love in a way that conquers pride and fear.

August 2

I hope to spend some time with you, if the Lord permits.

1 Corinthians 16:7

ear God, what joy we have in gathering to pray and praise you together. How encouraging it is to share what's happening on our separate life journeys and see your hand at work in so many different ways. Thank you for arranging those times of fellowship, Lord. They are blessed times indeed.

Grief can take care of itself, but to get the full value of joy you must have somebody to divide it with.

—Mark Twain

August 3

Unless the Lord builds the house, those who
build it labor in vain. Unless the Lord guards the city,
the guard keeps watch in vain. It is in vain that you
rise up early and go late to rest, eating the bread of
anxious toil; for he gives sleep to his beloved.

Psalm 127:1–2

Sometimes I try to do too much "building"
and "guarding" by my own efforts, Father.
Thank you for this reminder that everything I do to
further my own cause and ensure my own safety isn't
going to be effective apart from an abiding trust in
you. Help me remember, too, that you aren't just an
element of my life, like some add-on magic charm
to hedge all my bets. Forgive me for the times I've
treated you like that! You're no optional feature. You
are my provision and my protection—you are my very
life. Thank you for the peace of mind that always
comes when I stop trying to do it myself and tap into
your unending supply of strength.

August 4

*I have fought the good fight, I have finished
the race, I have kept the faith.*

2 Timothy 4:7

Lord, there comes a time in the life of every individual when she starts thinking less about "what I want to be when I grow up" and more about "finishing well." I want to finish well, Lord. Keep me strong and faithful to you until I draw my last breath! And most of all, keep me from wasting precious time between now and then. I want to keep running with you right up to the finish line.

God provides the wind, but man must raise the sails.

—Augustine of Hippo

August 5

Jesus said to the people who believed in him, "You are truly my disciples if you remain faithful to my teachings. And you will know the truth, and the truth will set you free."

John 8:31–32 NLT

What kind of freedom do you mean, Lord? There are people in jail cells in some countries because they have chosen to live according to your Word. Some of your other faithful followers struggle with illness or disability. So when you speak of freedom, you must mean something beyond a free body. I think you mean the spiritual freedom we enjoy in you. This freedom loosens any worldly bonds and holds the promise of eternal life in heaven. There the last vestiges of restraint will disappear, and our freedom will be complete.

The inner freedom we enjoy now in Christ is just a taste of what we will enjoy for all eternity.

August 6

Because your steadfast love is better than life,
my lips will praise you.

Psalm 63:3

Alleluia, Lord! How we praise you with our words, our songs, and our lives! When we look back over all the situations you've brought us through, we are so grateful. We are filled with confidence that we can face the future because you will be there with us. And so we just want to stop today and praise you for all you are and all you do! Alleluia and Amen!

Our joy is in our
praise of you,
oh Lord!

August 7

There is therefore now no condemnation for those who are in Christ Jesus. For the law of the Spirit of life in Christ Jesus has set you free from the law of sin and of death.

Romans 8:1–2

Lord, how I long to stand strong in the faith! I read of the martyrs of old and question my own loyalty and courage. Would I, if my life hung in the balance, say, "Yes, I believe in God"? I pray I would, Lord. Continue to prepare me for any opportunity to stand firm for what I know to be true. To live without conviction is hardly to live at all.

Be strong in the Lord in good times and hard times.

August 8

Then the Lord God will wipe away the tears from all faces.

Isaiah 25:8

A wise friend once gave me some advice I have come back to again and again over the course of my life. I was having trouble getting past some mistakes I had made, and my friend advised me to ask myself, "Am I feeling condemned by the devil, or am I being convicted by God's Spirit?" Condemnation, she told me, is never from God. "The devil will try to make you feel like you're just plain worthless," she said. "The Holy Spirit, by contrast, will direct you to confess your wrongdoing, receive God's forgiveness, make amends where you can, and get going in the right direction."

God never condemns his children. His gracious method is to get us back on track as quickly as possible.

August 9

*O give thanks to the Lord, for he is good;
for his steadfast love endures forever.*

1 Chronicles 16:34

Lord, today I want to give you thanks for all the little children who bring so much joy into the world. I feel that they must spring directly from your love for us. How we treasure the hugs and smiles of these little angels, Lord. They are as special to us as they are to you. Lay your hand upon their heads, Lord. Touch them with your grace, and keep them close to you.

*I love little children, and it is not
a slight thing when they,
who are fresh from God, love us.*

—Charles Dickens

August 10

Let the same mind be in you that was in Christ Jesus.

Philippians 2:5

Lord, how often we listen to the news
and we just don't know what to think.
We are shocked, confused, and sometimes terrified by
the things that are going on in the world around us.
Yet our first response should be, "What do *you* think,
Lord?" Please give us your insights on the events of
today, as we know nothing catches you by surprise.
Teach us to discern as you do, and help us see how we
can contribute to change things for the better.

*Let God change us
before we change
the world.*

August 11

*The Lord God helps me; therefore I have not been
disgraced; therefore I have set my face like flint, and I
know that I shall not be put to shame.*

Isaiah 50:7

ometimes doing the right thing takes
more guts than I'm able to muster, Lord.
If I do what I know I should, people might get angry
or exclude me. Help me, Lord! Give me the strength
of character to follow you, even when it makes me
unpopular for a while. I entrust the end result to you.

*Standing up for the truth might cost you in the moment,
but it'll pay dividends in the long run.*

August 12

But I trusted in your steadfast love; my heart
shall rejoice in your salvation. I will sing to the Lord,
because he has dealt bountifully with me.

Psalm 13:5–6

Lord, how grateful I am that, because
of your love for me, you have cleansed
me of my sin and offered me the gifts of forgiveness
and salvation with open arms. Never fail to nudge
me when I am starting down the wrong path, Lord.
I know your corrections are better than the world's
consequences.

God loves us just where we are,
but he also loves us too much to leave us there.

—Leighton Ford

August 13

Be filled with the Spirit, as you sing psalms
and hymns and spiritual songs among yourselves,
singing and making melody to the Lord in your hearts,
giving thanks to God the Father at all times and for
everything in the name of our Lord Jesus Christ.

Ephesians 5:18–20

Have you ever been overwhelmed with gratitude toward God? Ever started singing a favorite hymn or worship song just because you wanted to let God know how much you love him? That's the work of God's Spirit in us, filling us with praise, thanks, and love. These are precious offerings held in God's treasury of remembrance, just as we hold our own children's love gifts close to our hearts. Perhaps there is a love gift you would care to offer your heavenly Father even now as you consider his goodness.

You don't need to have perfect pitch to sing
praises to God. Many worshippers take great
comfort in the psalmist's mandate to make
a joyful noise to the Lord. Joyful noises from
attuned hearts are music to God's ears.

August 14

Let the favor of the Lord our God be upon us,
and prosper for us the work of
our hands—O prosper the work of our hands!

Psalm 90:17

ord, so often the difference between a productive workday and a fruitless one lies in our attitude. When we truly work as if working for you, it makes such a wonderful difference! Forgive us, Lord, for those times when we dig into our tasks without bringing you into the situation as well. Whether it's peeling potatoes, pulling weeds, or writing a screenplay, we want to tune into your power to perfect our work on this earth.

I have resolved to pray more and pray always,
to pray in all places where quietness inviteth:
in the house, on the highway and on
the street; and to know no street or passage
in this city that may not witness
that I have not forgotten God.

—Sir Thomas Browne

August 15

*I am the Lord your God; sanctify yourselves
therefore, and be holy, for I am holy.*

Leviticus 11:44

I used to think that *sanctify* meant something akin to "sanitize" when I was a young person. I thought God was calling me to clean up my act in this verse. But *sanctify* actually means "set apart," and in this case it means "set apart to God." It's a call for me to commit myself to God, to put myself in his hands, to be at his disposal, to be available for his purposes. Then, as I give myself to him, he helps me clean up my act and makes me able to walk in holiness.

*Lord, I choose to be set apart
as one who belongs to you,
is fully committed to you,
and is made holy by your
grace at work in my life.*

August 16

Now I know only in part; then I will know fully,
even as I have been fully known.

1 Corinthians 13:12

O Lord, how long the list of questions
I want to ask you in heaven is getting
to be! There are so many things that happen in life
that we just can't understand because we aren't able
to see them as completely as you do. Be patient with
our impatience, Lord. Help us remember that all the
answers will come to light on your schedule.

Our real blessings often appear to us in the shape of pains,
losses and disappointments; but let us have patience, and
we soon shall see them in their proper figures.

—Joseph Addison

August 17

You must understand this, my beloved: let everyone be quick to listen, slow to speak, slow to anger; for your anger does not produce God's righteousness.

James 1:19–20

Lord, I have had to experience this truth many times over. How many times has my anger produced regret, Father? More times than I can count. Thomas Jefferson advised counting to ten when angry and to a hundred when very angry. Too often, though, I'm more prone to Mark Twain's approach: "When angry, count four; when very angry, swear."

But I know that's not okay. I want to take the high road as often as possible. I want to be patient when frustrated, dignified when wronged. I confess my slowness to listen, my quickness to speak, and my habit of letting anger rule the moment. Here is a fresh start right now as I receive your forgiveness. Please lead me forward as one who is focused on following in your footsteps.

When you are offended at any man's fault, turn to yourself and study your own failings. Then you will forget your anger.

—Epictetus

August 18

For everything there is a season, and a time for every matter under heaven: a time to be born, and a time to die.

Ecclesiastes 3:1–2

There are few things in life more heartbreaking than the death of a child. One so recently born, exiting life far too soon for our hearts to handle it. A time to be born, and a time to die. But there's supposed to be lots of time in between—a lifetime, in fact. How do we pick up the pieces and go on when our hearts ache as they never have before?

O Lord, it is so hard to see the hope in certain circumstances. I guess we just need time. Time to grieve. Time to regain our balance. Time to renew our trust and hope for the future. While we are going through this season of healing, please hold us close.

And the mother gave, in tears and pain,
The flowers she most did love;
She knew she should find them all again
In the fields of light above.

—Henry Wadsworth Longfellow

August 19

Whenever you stand praying, forgive, if you have anything against anyone; so that your Father in heaven may also forgive you your trespasses.

Mark 11:25

Forgiveness is a supernatural response to being wronged. Would we know what forgiveness is if God had not shown us by first forgiving us? It seems highly unlikely. That's why real forgiveness—the kind that God extends to us—can only come through God's grace. In our own strength, we may try to forgive someone over and over again, only to call to mind the offense later (for perhaps the hundredth time). But when we ask God to open our hearts, he fills them with his love and makes us capable of full forgiveness.

Father, your forgiveness has transformed my life. Please fill my heart with love for those I have been reluctant to forgive.

August 20

*For I know that my Redeemer lives, and that at the last
he will stand upon the earth; and after my skin has been
thus destroyed, then in my flesh I shall see God.*

Job 19:25–26

ob spoke the words of the above passage
when his body was covered with painful
boils. After previously losing all his wealth and his
status, Job was enduring the deterioration of his
health while grieving over the loss of his children.
Job had always walked uprightly before God, and
all of these evils had befallen him nonetheless. How
disheartening! Still, even while Job was immersed
in pain and on the brink of death, his faith in God
did not waver. By focusing on his Redeemer and the
eternal life he knew was ahead for him, Job refused
to allow anything to rob him of his relationship
with God.

*Our pain may seem like
an indictment against God,
but our faith can get us
through all our difficulties.*

August 21

*This book of the law shall not depart out of
your mouth; you shall meditate on it day and night,
so that you may be careful to act in accordance with all
that is written in it. For then you shall make your way
prosperous, and then you shall be successful.*

Joshua 1:8

Lord, focusing on your Word is a great
blessing. The more I keep it before me,
the more faithfully I walk in your ways. Help me to
make the most of every opportunity I have to read,
think about,
and discuss the
things you share
with us through
the Scriptures.

*One should be just as careful in choosing one's
pleasures as in avoiding calamities.*

—Chinese Proverb

August 22

I know that whatever God does endures forever; nothing can be added to it, nor anything taken from it.

Ecclesiastes 3:14

Lord, in a world where everything seems to be here today and gone tomorrow, how wonderful it is to focus on the rich legacy we have in you. Everything you do and create lasts forever. How reassuring it is to accept that that means we will last forever too. Forever in your kingdom! Thank you, Lord.

There is one thing we trust in—the Lord, for he and his goodness are eternal.

August 23

*The Lord is slow to anger but great
in power... His way is in whirlwind and storm.*

Nahum 1:3

Lord, some days we turn on the news and it
seems as if you are turning the whole world
inside out. As horrified as we are by the devastation
of earthquakes, tornadoes, and floods, we need those
constant reminders that you are all powerful and
sovereign. Be merciful to us, O Lord. May we see you
at work in the wind and the waves and marvel at
your majesty.

*Praising God in the midst of a storm
is the best way to weather it.*

249

August 24

O Lord my God, I will give thanks to you forever.

Psalm 30:12

ord, so often it isn't until after a crisis has passed that we can see all the ways that you were present in the midst of it. Forgive us for focusing on the negative and missing your positive contributions. Remind us to expect your involvement— to actively watch for it, even! We need to be alert to the working of your Spirit in all things and give thanks at all times.

An easy thing, O power divine,
To thank Thee for these gifts of Thine,
For summer's sunshine, winter's snow,
For hearts that kindle, thoughts that glow;
But when shall I attain to this—
To thank Thee for the things I miss?

—Thomas Wentworth Higginson

August 25

Better is the end of a thing than its beginning; the patient in spirit are better than the proud in spirit.

Ecclesiastes 7:8

When I'm waiting through the turmoil of doing the right thing at the cost of my personal comfort, Lord, help me to be patient. Help me not to sabotage your works by trying to fix things in my own way. Oh, it's not always easy to hold my tongue, but if I wait until you open the door for me to speak—and I look to you for the right attitude when I do talk—then I won't have to deal with all the regrets and what-ifs. Grant me a patient spirit, Father.

God is my source for wisdom and courage.

251

August 26

Create in me a clean heart, O God, and put a new and right spirit within me.

Psalm 51:10

ord, a vexing situation has me very confused. Is it possible I'm trying to sort it out through my own limited understanding and overlooking a crucial element? I know I can trust you with anything. I give this up to you and ask you to restore me to a place where I can look at what's going on in the right way—*your* way.

Letting go is not giving up if you let go in order to grab the hand of God.

252

August 27

There is no Holy One like the Lord, no one besides you;
there is no Rock like our God.

1 Samuel 2:2

Lord, please keep me from falling into the trap of placing any other human on a pedestal. Even the most spiritual-seeming religious leaders are riddled with imperfection; they struggle with sin, just as I do. You alone are perfect and pure, and you alone are worthy of my adoration. I promise I will not follow anyone else, no matter how spiritually enlightened they may seem. There is no one like you, and you are the only one who will ever have my full devotion.

Greatness lies not in being strong, but in the right use of strength.
—Henry Ward Beecher

August 28

Keep your lives free from the love of money,
and be content with what you have; for he has said,
"I will never leave you or forsake you."

Hebrews 13:5

ather God, you are the giver of all gifts. All of our resources and all we have came from you, and they are only ours for a little while. Protect us from any addiction to material things, Lord. Gently remind us when we have enough—enough to eat, enough to wear, enough to enjoy. Most of all, keep us mindful of the fact that because we have you, we have everything we need.

I have lived through much and now I think I have found
what is needed for happiness. A quiet, secluded life in the
country with the possibility of being useful.

—Leo Tolstoy

August 29

The sacrifice acceptable to God is a broken spirit; a broken and contrite heart, O God, you will not despise.

Psalm 51:17

I am grateful that you don't require spiritual gymnastics from me when I sin, Lord. You just call me to come to you with a humble and repentant heart. In my pride I sometimes want to do something that will impress you—something that will "make up for it" somehow. But you just shake your head and keep calling me to humble myself and bring my sincere sorrow to you. That often doesn't seem like enough to me. But I guess that's the point: I can never earn your grace; it is a gift. Christ died on the cross for us because it is beyond our powers to make up for all the sins we have committed. I bring my contrite heart before you now, Lord. Thank you for receiving it as an acceptable sacrifice.

The first step in receiving God's grace is the realization that we need it.

August 30

*And this is my prayer, that your love may overflow
more and more with knowledge and full insight
to help you to determine what is best.*

Philippians 1:9–10

O Lord, how I pray for the young people
I love as they head out into the world
on their own. Help them tune in to your presence,
Lord, and make them wise beyond their years. Warn
them of dangers and protect them from the schemes
of others. Teach them to love themselves and others

extravagantly, but wisely
as well. They are your
children, Lord, and you
love them even more
than I do. I place them in
your hands.

*Wherever we go, echoes
of the voices of all who
have loved us provide the
rhythm for our steps.*

August 31

Rash words are like sword thrusts,
but the tongue of the wise brings healing.

Proverbs 12:18

nce that verbal barb is out there, there's no taking it back. It may have felt good for a moment, but the sense of triumph gives way almost immediately to a sense of regret. If wisdom rules our tongues, however, the sword of our words will defend and encourage those around us. It will secure honor and blessing by its careful use and make those around us feel secure rather than threatened.

Lord, guard my words! Keep my tongue in check, and help me wield it in ways that bring healing and peace to those around me today.

September

September 1

*Now to him who by the power at work within us
is able to accomplish abundantly far more than all we can
ask or imagine, to him be glory in the church and in Christ
Jesus to all generations, forever and ever. Amen.*

Ephesians 3:20–22

ather, sometimes I ask myself, *What good am
I doing on this earth?* I look at people who
seem to have found work perfectly suited to them,
and I wonder if I am fulfilling my purpose. Thank you
for this passage reminding me that you are at work
in me, bringing about your purposes, which are not
always clear to me. I need to remember that you are
working amazing things through even the tiniest acts.
You take small gifts—as you did with the loaves and
the fishes—and you cause them to multiply.

*Lord, help me not to look for
visible results as I serve you today.
Help me to focus on being faithful
in the little things and
to trust you with the big picture.*

September 2

You shall love the Lord your God
with all your heart, and with all your soul,
and with all your mind.

Matthew 22:37

ord, I want my love for you to be expressed
as naturally as breathing in and out. In that
way my whole existence—my very life itself—will be
an expression of my love for you. Accept my meager
attempts to love you completely, Lord.

What know we of the Blest above
But that they sing, and that they love.

—William Wordsworth

September 3

I thank my God every time I remember you, constantly praying with joy in every one of my prayers for all of you.

Philippians 1:3–4

Thank you for those who pray for me, Father. Thank you for putting me in their hearts and minds. I know that at times someone is keeping me in their prayers, and I haven't the faintest clue. It could be my hairdresser, chiropractor, pastor, or even someone I've just met. Perhaps a checker at the grocery store recalls a bit of conversation we had and now prays for me from time to time. You  work in such unusual ways that I never know how it might be happening—I just know that it is so, and I am grateful.

To be remembered in prayer is to be lifted up to God in a very special way. Is there someone God is bringing to my mind right now for prayer?

September 4

Welcome one another, therefore, just as Christ has welcomed you, for the glory of God.

Romans 15:7

ord, how grateful I am for the gift of hospitality. When others make me feel welcome in their home, it fills me with warmth and love. Help me to cultivate this gift in myself, Lord, so that those who enter my home may find sweet joy and hope.

Stay *is a charming word in a friend's vocabulary.*

—Louisa May Alcott

262

September 5

Do nothing from selfish ambition or conceit,
but in humility regard others as better than yourselves.
Let each of you look not to your own interests,
but to the interests of others.

Philippians 2:3–4

Weeks ago I was sitting at a table in a café that overlooked a lovely bay. It was a beautiful Saturday morning in late summer, and there were quiet conversations going on all around me. At one point, I could clearly hear a woman's voice above the quiet din. She was reciting her accomplishments—the people she'd managed, the boards she'd served on, and all the awards she'd received. Her boasting was jarring in the serene setting. I stole a glance over to her table to see if she was perhaps on a job interview. She didn't seem to be. I called to mind times when I felt the need to remind others of my importance, and I felt a twinge of guilt deep inside. How cloying such words must sound in God's ear.

Lord, forgive my self-important words
that serve only to distance me
from others and from you.
Let true humility always thrive in my life.

September 6

Whoever does not love does not know God, for God is love.

1 John 4:8

lmighty God, today I pray for all those who feel love has passed them by. Due to the circumstances of their lives, they can't think of even one person who truly loves them. How hard it must be to reach out and love others if you have never felt the warmth of love yourself. How that could all change if they come to know you, God! Reach through the loneliness with your love, Father.

The true measure of a man is how he treats someone who can do him absolutely no good.

—Samuel Johnson

September 7

How beautiful upon the mountains are the feet
of the messenger who announces peace, who brings
good news, who announces salvation.

Isaiah 52:7

ome feet are pretty, others are less so. The recently pedicured feet of a model are quite a contrast to the callus-ridden feet of the marathon runner. But from God's perspective, any foot that carries the message of love and peace is a thing of beauty. Let your feet be lovely today in the most meaningful sense as you bring showers of kindness wherever you go.

Whether I'm walking to the grocery store
or to give an important speech, Father,
help me remember what my feet are really for.

September 8

For everything created by God is good, and nothing is to be rejected, provided it is received with thanksgiving; for it is sanctified by God's word and by prayer.

1 Timothy 4:4–5

Does this apply to the most annoying gnats, Lord? What about mean people and cold-blooded killers? Sometimes it is hard to see the good. Help me to do my part with love, then pray over and give up the more confounding elements to you.

Saying a small prayer whenever we are troubled helps us remember that though there are many things beyond our grasp, all is in God's hands.

September 9

Now, discipline always seems painful rather than pleasant at the time, but later it yields the peaceful fruit of righteousness to those who have been trained by it.

Hebrews 12:11

Lord, we don't have to look far to see the proof of this verse. Take the difference between the person who received loving discipline from their parents and the one who didn't or refused to bend to it. The prudent, well-behaved individual exhibits a degree of self-control and self-respect that is lacking in the one who was never taught or who stubbornly disregarded all corrective measures. I'm your child, Lord. Grant me the grace to accept your discipline, even when it hurts. I trust your wisdom and love for me as you train me to live a more peaceful, productive life.

Parenting can be a thankless job . . . until the child grows up and begins to grasp the depth of the parent's love.

267

September 10

A cheerful heart is a good medicine,
but a downcast spirit dries up the bones.

Proverbs 17:22

Lord, how we thank you for the gift of laughter! Even in the midst of grief you send those happy memories that make us laugh and bring comfort to our souls. Laughter is so healing, Lord. It's reassuring to see so much evidence of your sense of humor. I feel confident there will be lots of laughter in heaven!

With the fearful strain that is on me night and day, if I did not laugh I should die.

—Abraham Lincoln

September 11

Jesus looked at them and said, "For mortals
it is impossible, but not for God;
for God all things are possible."

Mark 10:27

Lord, how hard it is for us all to live in peace
with one another. We all have our own ideas
about how the world should be, and some topics
can be polarizing. Help us to act in loving ways and
to work hard to see and respect others' points of
view. We all love this world and you—please help us
keep this in mind and work from there. It is easy to
get ahead of ourselves and lose hope; we also know,
though, that you are always present, and we truly
believe that anything is possible with you. We place
the troubles of our world at your feet. We know you
will mold them into something breathtaking.

Will you end wars by asking men to trust
men who evidently cannot be trusted? No.
Teach them to love and trust God; then they
will be able to love the men they cannot
trust, and will dare to make peace with
them, not trusting in them but in God.

—Thomas Merton

*In all these things we are more than conquerors
through him who loved us.*

Romans 8:37

Lord, today I pray for all those who are suffering from any sort of addiction. Whether it's drugs, gambling, overeating, or compulsive exercising, Lord, addiction keeps them from being the people you designed them to be. Their obsession separates them from you and walls them off from their loved ones as well. Break through and release

them from their chains, Lord. Give them the strength to put their troubles behind them and find new life in you.

*God make me brave—Life brings
Such blinding things,
Help me to keep my sight,
Help me to see aright
That out of dark—comes light.*

—Grace Noll Crowell

September 13

*Thus says the Lord: Stand at the crossroads, and look,
and ask for the ancient paths, where the good way lies;
and walk in it, and find rest for your souls.*

Jeremiah 6:16

Crossroads pop up from time to time in life. We sometimes feel anxiety during these transitional times because we are taking on new roles with unfamiliar responsibilities. One common life crossroads is starting a family. Often those who have strayed will come back to religion after having their own children. Perhaps this is because the new parents are unsure in their new roles, or perhaps they simply valued religious traditions during their own childhoods and want their children to have similar experiences. Whatever the reason, such life crossroads are excellent opportunities to come back to God if we have strayed too far from him.

*I pray that you would always bring
me back to you, Father, if I should
wander away from your paths. Let
the crossroads of my life always be
reminders of my need for you.*

271

September 14

As far as the east is from the west,
so far he removes our transgressions from us.

Psalm 103:12

Lord, when you promise us you have removed our sins from us, why do we dredge them up so we can wallow in regret and shame all over again? Keep us from wasting time and energy thinking about past mistakes, Lord. If they are no longer on your radar, they surely don't belong on ours. How blessed we are to have such a compassionate, forgiving God!

The greatest security against sin
is to be shocked at its presence.

—Thomas Carlyle

September 15

*O the depth of the riches and wisdom and
knowledge of God! How unsearchable are
his judgments and how inscrutable his ways!*

Romans 11:33

Almighty God, there are so many times
when we come before you and simply
confess, "We don't understand." Keep us from wasting
time trying to make sense
of the inscrutable! While
we never want to stop
mining your Word for
gems of knowledge, help
us find peace in the truths
we can fathom and trust
you with everything else.

*This is happiness; to be dissolved
into something complete and great.*

—Willa Cather

September 16

He changes times and seasons... he gives wisdom to the wise and knowledge to those who have understanding.

Daniel 2:21

Lord, sometimes I feel you've blessed me with all kinds of knowledge that no one is interested in hearing! Help me know when and how to share your wisdom with others. Help me to *show* others your truth, rather than just talk about it. You taught us by living out the truth, Lord. Help us to do the same.

The shortest answer is doing.

—English Proverb

274

September 17

Guard me as the apple of the eye;
hide me in the shadow of your wings.

Psalm 17:8

Whenever I think of how you cherish me, I am amazed, Father. It's good for me to stop and remember that you actually delight in me, that you gave your most precious sacrifice to save me, and that there is nothing you would withhold from me that would benefit my life.

I want to simply rest in the shade of your protective love right now as you impress your love on my heart.

To be quiet in the presence of God and allow
his love to wash over us is perhaps the most
effective way to calm fear and subdue anger.

September 18

Be kind to one another, tenderhearted, forgiving one another, as God in Christ has forgiven you.

Ephesians 4:32

Lord, why is it that we see the faults of others so clearly but ignore our own until the pile gets so big, we finally trip over it? We desire to be more gracious than we are, Lord. Just as you have showered us with kindness and forgiveness, help us to do the same for those around us. Speak to our hearts, Lord. Open them and fill them with compassion.

One word or a pleasing smile is often enough to raise up a saddened and wounded soul.

—Thérèse of Liseux

September 19

*You show me the path of life. In your presence
there is fullness of joy; in your right hand
are pleasures forevermore.*

Psalm 16:11

Those who don't know you are missing so
much, Lord! Life, joy, pleasures are in your
hand, and you are eager to give them as gifts to those
who come to you. I pray today for those who are lost
and searching. Please shine your grace to light their
way. Draw them to yourself as only you can.

*I've heard it said that
telling others about the
Lord doesn't need to be
complicated. Really, it's
much like one pauper
showing another
pauper where she has
found treasure.*

September 20

*Iron sharpens iron, and one person sharpens
the wits of another.*

Proverbs 27:17

Good friends make us better people by keeping
us sharp. If we allow our friends to challenge
our perspective, discuss the meaningful stuff of life,
and keep us accountable to what is true and right and
good, we understand the value of being sharpened.
And if we're willing to reciprocate—sometimes even
at the risk of hurting our friend out of a heart of
love for them—then we understand the value of being
good sharpeners.

It's true that this
sharpening process
isn't always pleasant,
but it's always good.
True friends embrace
this reality.

*Blessed is he who loves his brother as well when he is afar
off as when he is by his side, and who would say nothing
behind his back he might not, in love, say before his face.*

—Francis of Assisi

September 21

A new heart I will give you, and a new spirit I will put within you; and I will remove from your body the heart of stone and give you a heart of flesh.

Ezekiel 36:26

You fulfilled this promise, Lord, when you gave your Holy Spirit to live within those who dedicate their lives to you. Thank you for transforming my heart with your saving grace and for making me sensitive to your Word and your ways. You truly have brought my soul alive—as if from stone to living flesh.

The strongest evidence that God is real is in the lives of those who have been transformed by his love.

September 22

*To them God chose to make known how great
among the Gentiles are the riches of the glory of this
mystery, which is Christ in you, the hope of glory.*

Colossians 1:27

Lord, how it breaks my heart to see pain
and loneliness in someone's eyes. Because
of the unfolding of your miraculous plan to send your
Son to die for us, hopelessness should never take up
residence in us, Lord! We can be filled with your Spirit
so quickly if we just focus on you. Help me bring your
hope to those in despair, Lord.

*As long as we are breathing, it's not
too late to accept God into our lives.*

September 23

Beloved, let us love one another, because love is from God;
everyone who loves is born of God and knows God.

1 John 4:7

here will always be people who are difficult to love. Fortunately, the requirement to love others is not a mandate to *like* them. Love is a choice to act in loving ways, regardless of whether we actually feel loving toward a person at any given time. Sometimes, though, we are surprised by what love can bring about in our hearts. Perhaps we've known an acquaintance for years and one day we see a new side of her. The realization that she will likely become a lovely flower in our bouquet of friends brings us great joy.

To the Christian love is the works of love. Christ's love was not an inner feeling, a full heart and whatnot, it was the work of love which was his life.

—Søren Kierkegaard

September 24

The Lord has done great things for us, and we rejoiced.

Psalm 126:3

ord, how good have you been to me? Let me count the ways! In times of discouragement all I need to do is sit quietly and remember all the times in the past when you stepped in to set wrongs right, gave me a second chance, or showed up with a last-minute miracle. Lord, you are so good. May my faith never waver in view of all the wonders you have wrought!

. . . all is a miracle. The stupendous order of nature, the revolution of a hundred million worlds around a million stars, the activity of light, the life of all animals, all are grand and perpetual miracles.

—Voltaire

September 25

And the life I now live in the flesh I live by faith in the Son of God, who loved me and gave himself for me.

Galatians 2:20

Lord, how hopelessly aware we are of our earthly bodies. They develop creaks and frailties—not to mention weird bumps and lumps! But thanks to you, we are so much more than our bodies. For although we live in the flesh, we are filled with your Holy Spirit; the life we live is really you living out your life in us! Thank you for that perspective, Lord. It makes it so much easier to watch our earthly bodies begin to fail. How ready we will be to exchange them for the heavenly models!

Take my life and let it be consecrated Lord for Thee.

—Frances Ridley Havergal

September 26

You are a hiding place for me; you preserve me from trouble; you surround me with glad cries of deliverance.

Psalm 32:7

Lord, when there seems to be no easy way out of a tough situation, I turn to you. When relationships seem too difficult to navigate, I turn to you. When I fear for my safety or feel threatened by bodily harm, I turn to you. You, O Lord, are my sanctuary. With you I am always safe. I praise you for this night and day!

This world might take my body, but not my soul, which is my very essence. My soul is always safe with God.

September 27

Beloved, never avenge yourselves, but leave room
for the wrath of God; for it is written, "Vengeance is mine,
I will repay, says the Lord."... Do not be overcome by evil,
but overcome evil with good.

Romans 12:19, 21

When someone
pelts me with a
peashooter, Lord, my first
inclination is to pull out a
dodgeball and fire back. The
only thing about retaliation,
though, is that I never feel
better after having exacted
my revenge. In fact, I feel

ashamed when I return evil with evil. On the other
hand, there's something truly freeing about returning
evil with good. When I let that driver get ahead of me
even though I know he cut me off farther back, I feel
peaceful. When I pray for him, I feel an empathy rise
up for him—for what his life may be like, for how
stressed he might be for whatever reason.

When I leave justice in God's hands,
I am free to carry his peace in mine.

285

September 28

Let endurance have its full effect, so that you may be mature and complete, lacking in nothing.

James 1:4

Lord, we are a people in search of a shortcut. Give us the five-minute dinner preparation and the instant credit. But we know, because you are so clear about this in your Word, that a mature faith can't be achieved overnight. Give us patience to endure, Lord. We are determined to become the complete

individuals you intended us to be.

It takes a great deal of time and pressure for a piece of coal to become a diamond.

286

September 29

Owe no one anything, except to love one another;
for the one who loves another has fulfilled the law.

Romans 13:8

The obligation to live up to other people's expectations can be overwhelming, Lord. Sometimes I find myself trying to make everyone happy, though I know that's impossible.

Here is your answer to my dilemma: You call me to greet every person with a heart of love. I may not be able to give them everything they want, but I can love them. Loving them will help me figure out the next step. If they are disappointed in what I have to offer, help me leave responsibility for their feelings with them and not carry false guilt. I am glad to do what you need from me, Father. What you ask of me is not a to-do list, but a way of relating that always extends your love.

Feelings of guilt are a good indicator that we are overloaded. It's often possible to cut out trivial chores here and there or find a willing partner for a particularly time-consuming task.

September 30

Keep your heart with all vigilance,
for from it flow the springs of life.

Proverbs 4:23

Lord, many times I have asked you to protect my heart from wanton wanderings, and you have always aided me. How grateful I am for your help, Lord. Thank you for steering my heart toward only what is good and true. My heart is full of love for many people, but it only belongs to you.

A heart that beats for the Lord will beat forever.

October

October 1

*In your book were written all the days that were formed
for me, when none of them as yet existed.*

Psalm 139:16

ord, how I love to wake up to a cool, crisp
fall day with snowcapped mountains in the
distance and the blue sky above. On mornings like
this I think, *What a wonderful day to be alive!* I soon
realize, however, that I should see each day of my
life as an extraordinary gift. Help me to remember to
value each day, Lord. And may I find in each of them
a way to bring glory to you.

*Write it on your heart that every day
is the best day in the year.*

—Ralph Waldo Emerson

October 2

*I am the good shepherd. The good shepherd lays down
his life for the sheep.... No one takes it from me,
but I lay it down of my own accord.*

John 10:11, 18

love being part of your flock, Lord. I could
go on all day about your good care for
me, and I often see evidence of how well you care for
all the other members of your flock as well. You care
for us as no one else ever could. You send us constant
reminders that there is nothing you would withhold
from us—not even your own life—to keep us safe in
your love.

*The shepherd has chosen you as one of his own,
and he guards you with his very life.*

October 3

When you reap the harvest of your land, you shall not reap to the very edges of your field, or gather the gleanings of your harvest; you shall leave them for the poor and for the alien: I am the Lord your God.

Leviticus 23:22

You think of everything, Lord God. We are often baffled by how to care for the most vulnerable among us, but your solution is simple: When you go to gather the fruits of your labor, leave something behind! Once we have what we need, it should be easy to leave the rest for others.

Our treasure is the compassion we show others.

October 4

I will praise the name of God with a song;
I will magnify him with thanksgiving.

Psalm 69:30

ord, today I feel particularly grateful for my silly cats. What joy and companionship they bring me each day, Lord. I know you created them, and I can see a bit of your mystery and majesty in them. Thank you for populating our world with such lovable creatures.

All things bright and beautiful,
All creatures great and small,
All things wise and wonderful,
The Lord God made them all.

—Cecil Frances Alexander

October 5

Indeed, you are my lamp, O Lord,
the Lord lightens my darkness.

2 Samuel 22:29

When I leave you behind and try to go about my day without your guidance, Lord, it's like groping around in the dark. I stub my heart on relational issues. I trip over my ego. I bump into walls of frustration. I fall down the steps of my foolish choices. How much better to seek the light of your presence first thing and enjoy the benefit of having you illuminate each step of my day!

It is good to embrace a hope.

—Ovid

October 6

I will send down the showers in their season;
they shall be showers of blessing.

Ezekiel 34:26

ord, my heart overflows with gratitude for all
the blessings you have sent into my life. I am
cognizant of the fact that I am probably only aware
of a small percentage of them, though. You are such
a generous God; you shower us with such abundance.
I am grateful for it all, Lord.

Each of us has a soul, but we forget to value it.
We don't remember that we are creatures made
in the image of God. We don't understand
the great secrets hidden inside of us.

—Teresa of Avila

October 7

I acknowledged my sin to you, and I did not hide my iniquity; I said, "I will confess my transgressions to the Lord," and you forgave the guilt of my sin.

Psalm 32:5

Confessing our sin to God is like bursting into cool, refreshing air after being stuck a long time in a stifling, hot room. It frees our soul from the suffocating misery of pride, guilt, and pretense. Best of all, "coming clean" about our wrongdoing is the way back to right relationship with God. His merciful love grants us the forgiveness we so desperately need.

The only sin God cannot forgive is the one I neglect to bring before him.

October 8

God saw everything that he had made,
and indeed, it was very good.

Genesis 1:31

ord, the intricacies of your creation are amazing! We appreciate the glorious fall colors, the radiant sunsets, and the starlit nights. We watch the animal world in awe of the design of each creature. Everything you made is excellent, Lord. May we never take any part of your creation for granted.

Glorious indeed is the
world of God around us,
but more glorious the
world of God within us.
—Henry Wadsworth Longfellow

October 9

The end of the matter; all has been heard. Fear God, and keep his commandments; for that is the whole duty of everyone. For God will bring every deed into judgment, including every secret thing, whether good or evil.

Ecclesiastes 12:13–14

Many of us in this modern world prefer nutshell versions of things—CliffsNotes, abstracts, "just the facts, ma'am." Here in these two verses, wise King Solomon gives us his own nutshell version of what our existence is all about. After all his philosophizing and musing on life and its meaning, he boiled it down to two duties: (1) Fear God and (2) Obey his commands. Elsewhere in Scripture we learn that all God's commands can be "nutshelled" into two simple commands: (1) Love God with all our being and (2) Love others by treating them as we would want to be treated.

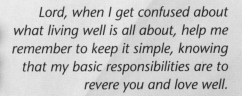

Lord, when I get confused about what living well is all about, help me remember to keep it simple, knowing that my basic responsibilities are to revere you and love well.

October 10

I came that they may have life, and have it abundantly.

Lord, sometimes I feel like we are all only living out a miniscule amount of the life you have offered us. Help us tap into your stream of living water on a regular basis. Teach us to live more courageously, love more extravagantly, and give more generously. We don't want life to pass us by. Keep us open to all you have wrapped up in this gift called life. And then one day, bring us into abundant life with you.

Life is what happens while you're busy making other plans.

—Anonymous

October 11

Are not five sparrows sold for two pennies?
Yet not one of them is forgotten in God's sight.
But even the hairs of your head are all counted. Do not be
afraid; you are of more value than many sparrows.

Luke 12:6–7

Father, I often need these assurances of your concern for me. Thank you for stating again and again in your Word that you love me and are looking after my well-being. Help me to take you at your word today and, in childlike trust, have confidence that you are always near.

I sing because I'm happy, I sing because I'm free,
For His eye is on the sparrow, and I know He watches me.

—Civilla D. Martin

October 12

But thanks be to God, who gives us the victory through our Lord Jesus Christ.

1 Corinthians 15:57

Lord, many of us would be rendered totally ineffective by the sins we have committed were it not for your gift of salvation. None of us would be of use to this world without your intervention. We need to acknowledge your victory over sin and death every day! The news of our salvation is too wonderful to keep to ourselves.

If you cannot preach like Peter,
If you cannot pray like Paul,
You can tell the love of Jesus,
And say, "He died for all."

—Traditional Spiritual

October 13

Come now, . . . says the Lord: though your sins are like scarlet, they shall be like snow; though they are red like crimson, they shall become like wool.

Isaiah 1:18

Lord, it's hard for me to conceive of how thoroughly you forgive me when I confess my sins to you. The stains on my soul are washed away, and you give me a fresh, clean start. Even though it's hard for me to wrap my understanding around this, please help me wrap my faith around it so I can believe that you completely forgive me.

Though we sometimes must endure consequences for wrongdoing, God never holds our sins against us. He forgives completely the moment we confess sincerely.

October 14

It is the Lord who goes before you. He will be
with you; he will not fail you or forsake you.
Do not fear or be dismayed.

Deuteronomy 31:8

Lord, how often we get bogged down in the "what-ifs" of an opportunity instead of trusting you and moving forward. Teach us to look at the big picture, Lord—to catch the vision of what you want to accomplish through us. Then give us the courage to move forward in faith, knowing that you will be with us.

No matter how far we travel, the Lord is already there.

October 15

*For my thoughts are not your thoughts, nor are
your ways my ways, says the Lord. For as the heavens are
higher than the earth, so are my ways higher than your
ways and my thoughts than your thoughts.*

Isaiah 55:8–9

Father, I am so grateful that your thoughts
and your ways go so far beyond my own!
Things in my life can be going along smoothly—and
I may think I have everything under control—but
it can all change in the blink of an eye. Help me
stay connected with you, Lord, so that whether I'm
enjoying smooth sailing or enduring high seas, I'll
know I'm held fast by you.

*Even if you had the most
able doctors, the strongest
bodyguards, the wisest
counselors, and the most
loving family in your corner,
everything they could offer
could not surpass what God
is able to provide.*

October 16

O Lord, you will hear the desire of the meek;
you will strengthen their heart, you will incline your ear
to do justice for the orphan and the oppressed.

Psalm 10:17–18

Lord, today I ask you to slow me down and open my ears so I will notice the needs of those around me. Too often I breeze by people with an offhand greeting but remain in a cocoon of my own concerns. I know many around me are hurting, Lord. Help me find ways to be of service.

If we were supposed to talk more than we listen,
we would have two mouths and one ear.

—Mark Twain

October 17

My grace is sufficient for you,
for power is made perfect in weakness.

2 Corinthians 12:9

Lord, do you have a victory song you sing over me when your ways triumph in my life? Do you exult when your truth and love prevail in me and you put down those age-old enemies of bitterness, hatred, resentment, and the like? I sometimes forget that you are not just calm and stoic. You rejoice over my victories and you grieve when I wander away from you. You welcome me with gladness as I come to you today, and you renew me in your love. You are truly wonderful to me, Lord.

The author of life is, himself, very much alive, and he has a vested interest in the lives of his beloved children.

October 18

*Be merciful to me, O God, be merciful to me, for in you
my soul takes refuge; in the shadow of your wings I will
take refuge, until the destroying storms pass by.*

Psalm 57:1

Lord, we should not just *turn* to you in times
of trouble, we should *run* to you. Where else
can we find both shelter and consolation? Where else
can we feel both completely safe and unconditionally
loved? Thank you for opening your arms to us
whenever we need to run into them. Help us learn
to run to you at the first sign of trouble. You are an
unfailing refuge.

*Better a stormy day with the Lord
than a sunny one far from him.*

Although you have not seen [Jesus], you love him; and even though you do not see him now, you believe in him and rejoice with an indescribable and glorious joy.

1 Peter 1:8

Jesus said that those who would believe in him without having seen him would be blessed. We get a glimpse of that blessing here in Peter's words of encouragement to the church. It is a blessing to live in such joy. People can work a lifetime to amass money and all the things it can buy without feeling such true joy. Yet those who trust in Christ have an abiding, "indescribable and glorious" joy that fills their innermost being. This doesn't mean we spend all our moments singing tra-la-la, though. It means that even on our most trying days, we land on hope instead of despair, love instead of hate, and peace instead of anxiety. Our joy in belonging to Christ—in having an eternal hope—trumps every trial.

Lord Jesus, thank you for the joy that belonging to you brings to my life. In you I have all I need.

October 20

Be still, and know that I am God! I am exalted
among the nations, I am exalted in the earth.

Psalm 46:10

Lord, it often happens that you are trying to
communicate an important truth to us, but
we are so busy searching for the truth elsewhere that
we don't stop and listen. Teach us the importance of
being still, Lord. Only when we are still can we be
aware of your presence and hear your voice. Only
when we quiet the stirrings of our own souls can we
connect with your will! Speak to us, Lord—and help us
be ready to listen.

No sound is sweeter than the voice of God.

October 21

Blessed are the peacemakers,
for they will be called children of God.

Matthew 5:9

ather, you are the greatest of all
peacemakers. You made reconciliation
with humanity possible by means of great personal
sacrifice—but without compromising the truth. Show
me how to follow your example today. Help me not to
settle for fake peace—the kind that comes when lies
are allowed to prevail for the sake of avoiding conflict.
Instead, grant me the courage, grace, and wisdom to
work toward real peace, which values all people and
fulfills our need for truth and love.

Peace prevails
when individuals
value the needs
and ideas of
others as much
as their own.

October 22

May those who sow in tears reap with shouts of joy.

Psalm 126:5

Lord, some days it seems that every hour is spent in toil, with little time left over for relaxing with loved ones. Help us keep in mind that our hours of work sow seeds of hope. In time, you will comfort us and restore us to a posture of joy and celebration. Thank you, Lord, for understanding both our need to work hard and our need to enjoy this beautiful life.

Only God can replace grief with pure joy!

October 23

Cast all your anxiety on him, because he cares for you.

1 Peter 5:7

Fretting produces nothing but overblown what-if scenarios in our minds. We end up suffering appetite loss when we need to be keeping up our strength and sleeplessness when we should be resting. How do we get off this treadmill of worry? We do just what this verse tells us to do: We take our big ol' bundle of fears and frets and hand them over to God. We say, "This is obviously too much for me to handle. Please help me with this situation, Lord." We know that if we do this, it will all work out for the best on God's timetable.

Lord, I might have to remind myself 100 times today to leave my cares with you, but each reminder will help make it a habit. Soon I will need to remind myself only 50 times, and it won't be long until I won't need any reminders—I'll simply know that you're in control, and all will come to fruition on your schedule.

October 24

Rejoice in hope, be patient in suffering, persevere in prayer.

Romans 12:12

Lord, sometimes I feel like throwing in the towel. I have so many responsibilities, and it is hard to keep up. Some days I juggle everything flawlessly, but then *one of those days* comes along. I oversleep, and I rush to drop the kids off at school. I arrive at work late, only to realize we have a meeting with an important client, and I am woefully unprepared. I finally get home after working late, and I am met with the news that one of my children is in trouble at school. I feel like a failure on days like this, Lord. Comfort me and fill me with the hope that only you can give. Give me the strength to keep going even when it's hard, so I can revel in the growth that results.

It's always too early to quit.
—Norman Vincent Peale

October 25

*Forgive, and you will be forgiven; give, and it will be given
to you. A good measure, pressed down, shaken together,
running over, will be put into your lap; for the measure
you give will be the measure you get back.*

Luke 6:37–38

A lot of people these days call it karma, Lord,
but I know the laws of justice and reward
aren't really controlled by some vague universal force.
You, the living God, declare that you are at work,
giving abundantly to those who follow in your ways.
You see everything we do—you see the times when we
are generous to others as well as the times when we
foolishly put ourselves first. You advise us to follow
in your ways because it is right and good, and you
promise abundant rewards. Whether our reward will
come soon after a good deed or later in heaven is
a mystery, but I trust you with this mystery, Lord.
I know your ways are true, noble, and good, and
through them, we will have all
we could ever long for.

*When we work in the spirit of
generosity, our labors certainly
have God's blessing.*

October 26

I praise you, for I am fearfully and wonderfully made.
Wonderful are your works; that I know very well.

Psalm 139:14

Lord, what a miracle each newborn baby is. We marvel at the tiny hands and rosebud lips, and we know such a masterpiece could only come from you! We pray for all little children today, Lord. Watch over them and guide their parents. Grant all parents the courage, strength, and wisdom they need to fulfill their sacred duties.

Though tears and fears may come our way, Pray for your children each and every day.

October 27

Blessed are the pure in heart,
for they will see God.

Matthew 5:8

How can I be pure in heart, Lord? I certainly don't always have right thoughts and motives. Perhaps being pure in heart can happen through being honest about what's going on inside my heart and working to purify it. I can make it a point to focus on what is right and true and good, continually turning my heart toward you to find those things and be renewed in them. That's why I'm here right now, Lord. Purify my heart as I walk close to you today and enjoy the blessing of fellowship with you.

Often it's when we begin thinking we have it all together spiritually that we really need to stop and take stock of our life. Understanding our need for God and how far short we all fall of his perfection keeps us near him and safe.

October 28

Do you not know that you are God's temple
and that God's Spirit dwells in you?

1 Corinthians 3:16

Lord, sometimes I wonder what you think of this temple you created. There are some leaks in the roof and a few cracks in the walls. I have not always treated my body as a sacred temple for your Spirit. I've had days where I've felt deflated and I've found refuge in a few too many chocolates or a few too many sips of wine. Yet I know that even when I falter, your beautiful Spirit does not abandon ship! May I focus on that truth, Lord, and strive to be the being you want me to be.

If only all the mirrors we gaze into would reflect our souls instead of just superficial imperfections.

October 29

I am the bread of life. Whoever comes to me will never be hungry, and whoever believes in me will never be thirsty.

John 6:35

ou truly do satisfy my spiritual hunger, Lord! In fact, when I'm away from you due to distractions or detours of my own making, I deeply feel the lack of you in my life. But then when I stop and take time to "feed" on your Word and spend time "drinking in" your comfort, I am strengthened and refreshed again. How true your Word is!

When Jesus was teaching his followers to pray, he told them to ask, "Give us this day our daily bread." This certainly includes our spiritual sustenance as well as our daily meals.

October 30

The beginning of wisdom is this: Get wisdom.
Though it cost all you have, get understanding.

Proverbs 4:7 NIV

ord, sometimes it's hard for us to discern the difference between brave, courageous actions and foolish, faulty ones. Often we rush ahead with a plan we think is from you only to watch it end in disaster. At these times we know we moved too fast. Yet we don't want to lack the faith to move forward when necessary! Give us wisdom and discernment, Lord. Let the courageous spirit you instilled in us fuel actions that bring you glory.

Wisdom outweighs
any wealth.
—Sophocles

October 31

O give thanks to the Lord, for he is good;
his steadfast love endures forever!

Psalm 118:1

Lord, how grateful I am for the wise leaders who came before me. Reading old journals, books, and accounts of their lives, I see how you were as active in their lives as you are in ours today. Reading about the past gives us hope and innovation for the future, and we come away reassured that you are always with us. Thank you, Lord, for your steadfast love through all generations.

O God, our help in ages past, our hope for years to come.

—Isaac Watts

November

Again Jesus spoke to them, saying, "I am the light
of the world. Whoever follows me will never walk in
darkness but will have the light of life."

John 8:12

There's a path straddling the Montana-Idaho
border—an old railroad bed that's been
converted into a "rail trail" for bicycles. This fifteen-
mile stretch is touted as "one of the most breathtaking
scenic stretches of railroad in the country," with seven
high spans and ten tunnels. One of these tunnels
stretches for nearly two miles. Without a bicycle
light, it would be virtually impossible to ride through
without falling or crashing. A lightless rider's best
hope would be to find another rider with a light and
ride very close to that individual.

Life, too, is beautiful in places, but it can also be
treacherous. The best way to make it through is by
staying close to Jesus, the light of the world.

*Lord Jesus, thank you for your light, which
leads me through the darkness and lights
my way home to you.*

November 2

Learn to do good; seek justice, rescue the
oppressed, defend the orphan, plead for the widow.

Isaiah 1:17

ord, teach me how to help and defend the
vulnerable people around me—the children,
the sick, the infirm, the elderly, the poor. They are
easily taken advantage of by those more powerful
than they are, but I know you have a special place
in your heart for them. Help me not to look the
other way when intervening would be inconvenient
or scary. Grant me your wisdom, insight, and grace
to effectively help
wherever and
whenever I can.

Learning to do good for
the sake of others is one
of life's most fulfilling
endeavors.

November 3

Therefore, my beloved, be steadfast, immovable, always excelling in the work of the Lord, because you know that in the Lord your labor is not in vain.

1 Corinthians 15:58

Sometimes, Father, I feel like I don't get any credit for the work I do in your name. Help me to remember that the ultimate worth of the work I do is not in how others see it but in my doing it to please you. If you are pleased, then I have done well. Help me to move forward joyfully in my work as I focus on you today.

If others fail to encourage me, let me not fail to encourage them—to love others as I would want to be loved.

November 4

But these are written so that you may come to believe that Jesus is the Messiah, the Son of God, and that through believing you may have life in his name.

John 20:31

Lord, how many lives have been changed by the reforming, transforming power of your Word! So often I stumble upon a common verse, and it strikes me in a new, wonderful way. It brings breathtaking clarity when I need it most. Thank you for giving us your Word, Lord. We would be lost without it.

Far better it would be to take a few hours from active life and spend it in communion with God, than to be busy about many things while neglecting the one thing that is necessary for peace and happiness.

—Fulton Sheen

325

November 5

I am the way, and the truth, and the life.
No one comes to the Father except through me.

John 14:6

esus was the fulfillment of God's promise
of salvation. His life and death made
salvation possible for us. What a glorious, selfless gift!
I ponder this blessing every day, and gratitude and joy
fill my very being.

What is a charitable heart? It is the heart
of him who burns with pity for all creation.

—Isaak of Syria

November 6

Then little children were being brought to him in order that he might lay his hands on them and pray.

Matthew 19:13

O Lord, what a blessing children are in this world. They bring such joy into our lives and are a precious composite of the best of our past and the hopes for the future. Thank you for your love for all children, Lord. Please guard them always.

The laughter of a child is the light of a house.

—African Proverb

I am the vine, you are the branches. Those who abide in me and I in them bear much fruit, because apart from me you can do nothing.

John 15:5

ord, please help me to remember that you are the source of all good things that come out of my life as I grow and flourish in you. All the "good fruit" of love, joy, peace, patience, kindness, goodness, faithfulness, gentleness, and self-control come directly from you and then produce good things in me. I want to thank you for nourishing and supporting my life. Please use the fruit you're producing in me to nourish others and lead them to you as well.

Staying connected to the true Vine is the most important thing I'll do today.

November 8

*May the God of peace himself sanctify you entirely;
and may your spirit and soul and body be kept sound and
blameless at the coming of our Lord Jesus Christ. The one
who calls you is faithful, and he will do this.*

1 Thessalonians 5:23–24

Maybe it's bitterness. Maybe it's timidity. Maybe it's pride. Or maybe we tend to gossip or complain. Whatever sins we struggle with, though, we should never lose heart! Often it's our weaknesses that keep us close to God. When we find ourselves overwhelmed

with feelings of bitterness, it's a signal that we're not devoting enough time to prayer and reflection. God is faithful, and it's only through him that we can overcome our weaknesses. So rather than becoming discouraged that we still have the same old struggles, we need to look at our struggles as strings binding us to our heavenly Father.

*Lord, I need you today. I need you all day, every day.
Thank you for your faithfulness.*

November 9

*Do not be conformed to this world, but be
transformed by the renewing of your minds,
so that you may discern what is the will of God—what is
good and acceptable and perfect.*

Romans 12:2

When I have one foot in the worldly scene
and one foot in your kingdom, Lord, I'm
compromising. Your ways of humility, love, and
forgiveness are so at odds with worldly material
values that there is no way to play both fields at
once. I have a choice to make. Do I choose to indulge
in a lifetime of hedonistic pleasures, or will I choose
to serve you, walking in your peaceful ways now
and looking forward to the promise of eternity? I
know what I choose, Lord. That's why I'm spending
time with you right
now. Help me to walk
uncompromised today.

*You can't sit on
two chairs at once.*
—Dutch Proverb

November 10

Rejoice with those who rejoice, weep with those who weep.

Romans 12:15

Lord, so often when someone dies, the tears and the laughter get all mixed up together. The absence of the person makes us reflect on the good times we shared with them, and laughter interrupts our tears. I think that's your way of helping us begin to heal, Lord. Help us to revel in the laughter when it comes and let the tears flow when necessary too. If we lean on each other and on you,

we can move through grief in a life-affirming way, with our cherished memories intact.

Lord, we do not complain because you have taken him from us, but rather we thank you for having given him to us.

—Angelo Sodano

November 11

Grow in the grace and knowledge of our Lord and Savior Jesus Christ.

2 Peter 3:18

Growing in the *grace* of Christ is to embrace all that he freely offers me in the way of love, mercy, and salvation. And as I grow in his grace, I'll get better and better at extending love and mercy to others. To grow in the *knowledge* of Christ is to spend time with him in prayer and worship. As I spend more time with him, it will get easier and easier to follow the example he set for us.

Lord Jesus, you are worth knowing, worth emulating, worth every moment I spend seeking you out. Help me grow more like you as I walk in fellowship with you today.

November 12

But ask the animals, and they will teach you;
the birds of the air, and they will tell you.

Job 12:7

ord, how grateful I am that I once again
notice the lovely animals all around me.
There was a time in my life when I was so busy,
I didn't see them at all, though I know they were
always there. Now the birds, the deer—even the

raccoons—bring me
joy every day as I
watch them from
my office window.
Catching precious
glimpses of these
creatures of yours
helps me value
every moment of
every day.

A lifetime is made up of moments well lived.
Be present in each precious moment.

November 13

Indeed, rarely will anyone die for a righteous person—though perhaps for a good person someone might actually dare to die. But God proves his love for us in that while we still were sinners Christ died for us.

Romans 5:7–8

No one can touch your track record of love, Lord. How is it, then, that I find myself doubting that you can or will love me at times? Forgive me when I project my own inept love abilities onto you. Also, beyond learning to accept your great love, Lord, help me grow in it and become more and more able to love others—even when I am unloved by them.

To have courage for whatever comes in life— everything lies in that.

—Teresa of Avila

November 14

*I am grateful to God...when I remember you
constantly in my prayers night and day.*

2 Timothy 1:3

*L*ord, we are so thankful to you for our
families and close friends. How lonely our
lives would be without them, even in this splendid
world of your making! What a privilege it is to come
to you every day to offer prayers for them. Day after
day I bring before you those close to me who need
your special attention. If I can't sleep at night, I pray
for them again. Each one
is so precious to me, Lord,
and I know you cherish
them as well. As I think of
them during the day, please
consider each thought to
be another small prayer.

*People whose faith is unaffected and who are convinced
that petitions are always heard, and often granted,
bring their needs before God in the same matter-of-fact,
unembarrassed fashion as they ask a request of a friend.*

—Arnold Lunn

November 15

Peter said to [the crowd], "Repent, and be baptized
every one of you in the name of Jesus Christ
so that your sins may be forgiven;
and you will receive the gift of the Holy Spirit."

Acts 2:38

Father, you're always calling to us to turn our
backs on sin and turn our faces toward you.
You even promise to give us your own Spirit to lead
and guide us and strengthen us to walk in your ways.
I praise you today for your tireless love and concern
for all people
and for reaching
out to us with
your message of
salvation.

You must accept your cross; if you carry it
courageously it will carry you to heaven.

—John Vianney

November 16

*Do not neglect to show hospitality to strangers,
for by doing that some have
entertained angels without knowing it.*

Hebrews 13:2

ord, even when I'm tired and have too much to do, give me your spirit of graciousness during the coming holiday season. Allow me to open my heart to all those I encounter and to treat each visitor to my home as an honored guest. Most of all, let me be hospitable without regard to whether the person will ever return the favor. I want to greet everyone as you would greet them, Lord—with compassion and an unconditional welcome.

As soon as there is room for God in our soul, there is room for all those persons who have really a claim on our heart.

—Vincent McNabb

November 17

So we do not lose heart. Even though our outer nature is wasting away, our inner nature is being renewed day by day.

2 Corinthians 4:16

Little changes become apparent from year to year in this life. Maybe there's an extra pound or two on our frame. Maybe we've spotted a new gray hair (or two or twenty). Perhaps we suddenly realize we're taking things a little more slowly. As women who belong to God, though, we know these changes are trivial in light of eternity. As our bodies begin to show signs of age, our inner self is growing in radiance, compounding in beauty, flourishing in faith. We are just beginning to blossom within, just beginning to display a bit of the brightness that will burst forth in heaven when our life is finally fully opened to the light of God's love.

Lord, help me to live in light of eternity today, focusing more on my inner nature than on my outer appearance.

November 18

*Better is a dry morsel with quiet than
a house full of feasting with strife.*

Proverbs 17:1

Lord, it gets so crowded when everyone's home for the holidays—and there can be strife! It's easy for us to long for a quick return to our quieter day-to-day lives. Don't let our desire for peace and quiet rob us of the joy of spending time with loved ones, Lord! You've blessed us with quiet times and celebratory times, and we want to make the most of both.

*A house overflowing with loved ones
is a house overflowing with blessings.*

November 19

The fruit of the Spirit is love, joy, peace,
patience, kindness, generosity, faithfulness, gentleness, and
self-control. There is no law against such things.

Galatians 5:22–23

The people I know who walk in the ways of God are savory with the fruit of God's Spirit; they're the kind of people I can't be around enough. Their kind and gentle ways radiate peace. Their joy is contagious. Their faithfulness is inspiring. So many things about them make me want to be more like them—and more like Christ.

Lord, lead me by your Spirit
today, so that the fruit of my
character will bear witness to
my genuine faith in you.

November 20

*What woman having ten silver coins, if she loses
one of them, does not light a lamp, sweep the house,
and search carefully...? When she has found it, she calls
together her friends and neighbors, saying, "Rejoice with
me, for I have found the coin that I had lost." Just so,
I tell you, there is joy in the presence of
the angels of God over one sinner who repents.*

Luke 15:8–10

These verses fill my heart with hope, Lord.
Sometimes—when I'm lost on this path of
life—I sense your presence. It is so comforting to think
of you searching tirelessly to find me again. Grant me
your grace so I can stay on your paths more steadily.
This way, you'll have more time to devote to searching
out others!

*God doesn't give
up on anyone.
He loves all his
children and is at
work in their hearts
in ways no one else
can see.*

November 21

If we live by the Spirit, let us also be guided by the Spirit.

Galatians 5:25

Thank you, Father, for your Holy Spirit, who guides me through each day. May I willingly follow his lead, no matter when or where. Help me to obey quickly when he directs me to serve or forgive others. May I always be thankful and rejoice in the blessings he points out to me along the way.

May we set aside many moments throughout our busy days to tune in to God's Spirit and discern his plans for us.

November 22

And God is able to provide you with every blessing in abundance, so that by always having enough of everything, you may share abundantly in every good work.

2 Corinthians 9:8

Lord, as we enter this season of thanksgiving, how important it is for us to grasp the concept of "enough." You know how this world tempts us with all that is bigger, better—more in every way! But there is such joy and freedom in trusting that you will give us exactly what we need—neither too little nor too much. May we never take for granted all the blessings we have, Lord, and may we be as generous with others as you are with us. It is the simple life that brings us closest to you; we are blessed when we live simply.

Find out how much God has given you and from it take what you need; the remainder is needed by others.

—Augustine of Hippo

November 23

*For by grace you have been saved through faith,
and this is not your own doing; it is the gift of God—not
the result of works, so that no one may boast.*

Ephesians 2:8–9

ord, I am grateful that you don't have a list
of criteria for being eligible for salvation.
What insecurity that would create in us! I feel blessed
that I don't need to resort to servile fear or self-
important boasting when it comes to my standing
with you. Your salvation is a gift available to all and
secured by your merits (not mine). It is received only
by grace through faith in you.

*The playing field is
leveled when we stand
before God to give an
account of our imperfect
lives. But our champion
is Jesus—our perfect
brother—who credits his
own righteousness to our
accounts if we welcome
him into our lives.*

344

November 24

Deliverance belongs to the Lord;
may your blessing be on your people!

Psalm 3:8

Lord, no matter what our personal battles are this holiday season, we rest assured that you are with us every moment. Family relationships can be strained this time of year. Feelings can be easily trampled. But what better time to focus on all the blessings we have (even if some of them come in the form of difficult relatives!). Deliver us from any ill will, Lord, and keep us focused on all the reasons we have to be thankful.

Reflect on your present blessings, of which every man has many; not on your past misfortunes, of which all men have some.

—Charles Dickens

November 25

Clothe yourselves with compassion, kindness, humility, meekness, and patience. Bear with one another and, if anyone has a complaint against another, forgive each other; just as the Lord has forgiven you, so you also must forgive.

Colossians 3:12–13

hen others harm us, there is a path to healing that should include confession by the guilty party, actions that restore where possible, and a change of behavior that demonstrates genuine repentance. Meanwhile, whether or not the other party does what is right, we can choose to forgive. Instead of choosing retaliation or revenge, we can extend love and compassion. This doesn't mean that we coddle them or fail to confront any hurtful ways, but it does mean that even as we hold them accountable, we don't withhold our love.

Forgiveness is the fragrance the violet sheds on the heel that has crushed it.

—Mark Twain

November 26

*Take delight in the Lord, and he will give you
the desires of your heart.*

Psalm 37:4

Lord, how wonderful are your promises!
But because I trust your heart more
than my own, I only want to receive the desires of
my heart if they are desires that originate with you.
Teach me to know the difference, Lord—the difference
between fleeting, worldly desires and those that have
your blessing. Then, Lord—and only then—give me the
desires of my heart.

Lord, if this be your will, so let it be.

—Thomas à Kempis

November 27

*And now, our God, we give thanks to you
and praise your glorious name.*

1 Chronicles 29:13

Lord, how important it is for us to be
thankful at all times. It's so easy to fall
into the trap of having specific expectations and then
despairing when events take an unexpected turn.
You are working in our lives every moment, Lord.
We will do our part by working hard and taking full
advantage of all opportunities
that come our way, but we
also know that some matters
are reserved for you. We are
thankful that nothing is beyond
your control, Lord, and we are grateful that you are
our wise leader.

*Lord, behold our family here assembled. We thank you
for this place in which we dwell, for the love that
unites us, for the peace accorded us this day, for the hope
with which we expect the morrow; for the health, the
work, the food and the bright skies that make our lives
delightful; for our friends in all parts of the earth.*

—Robert Louis Stevenson

November 28

The Lord watch between you and me,
when we are absent one from the other.

Genesis 31:49

Lord, how hard it is to say good-bye to loved ones visiting from thousands of miles away. Help us be mindful that even on days when we can't see their smiles or feel their hugs, you are lovingly watching over all of us. We are connected in a special way through you, Lord. Spiritually, we are never far apart.

If you pray for me and I pray for you, God closes the distance between us two.

November 29

*Wait for the Lord; be strong, and let your heart
take courage; wait for the Lord!*

Psalm 27:14

Lord, what a blessing to be entering the
Advent season and prayerfully considering
the joyous celebration of your birth. Don't let us get
so bogged down by minutiae that we miss the miracle,
Lord. Prepare our hearts as we prepare our homes and
families for Christmas, and help us keep our focus not
on everything we need to do, but on you.

Just when we need it the most, Christmas enters our world.

November 30

Take my yoke upon you, and learn from me;
for I am gentle and humble in heart,
and you will find rest for your souls.

Matthew 11:29

Lord, if ever there was a day when I needed your rest, it is today. Just carrying around my to-do list is exhausting—it is so long! Help me sort out which things really need to be done and which I can let go. Stay particularly close to me in the coming weeks, Lord. I need your holy perspective.

A wise woman trades her to-do list for the Lord's.

December

December 1

Humble yourselves before the Lord, and he will exalt you.

James 4:10

The world we live in celebrates stardom, and the seemingly logical course of action is to promote ourselves like crazy to make sure we get our slice of the fame-and-fortune pie. James's advice, however, sounds more like a serving of humble pie; who wants to eat that? That'll get you exactly nowhere.... Or so we may think. But, case in point, Jesus humbled himself in the most profound way, and the outcome of his humility is reigning forever as King of Kings and Lord of Lords.

We don't need to be afraid of walking in quietness and obscurity as we serve God with sincere hearts. He remembers every faithful step of our journey, and one day—whether on this side of eternity or the other—he will commend us.

We shall not grow wiser before
we learn that much that
we have done was very foolish.

—F. A. Hayek

December 2

To the King of the ages, immortal, invisible, the only God,
be honor and glory forever and ever. Amen.

1 Timothy 1:17

Sometimes it's good for me to just step back and look at the whole picture of who you are, Lord—to remember your greatness and meditate on all the implications of it. When I look at how big you are, my problems that seemed so gigantic a few moments ago suddenly seem almost silly. My big plans seem less important, and my high notions of myself get cut down to size. I come away not feeling diminished, though—rather lifted up in spirit and full of faith and gratitude. Surely we were made to praise you, Lord!

Bringing honor
and glory to
God's name is our
greatest calling,
our highest
purpose, and our
most fulfilling
endeavor.

December 3

I will both lie down and sleep in peace; for you alone,
O Lord, make me lie down in safety.

Psalm 4:8

How restful it is to live in your love, Lord God! In the middle of chaos or turmoil, I remember that you are with me, and I am at peace once again. When it seems as if everything is falling apart, you hold me close in your love, and I am able to sleep at night. There is no other source of peace like belonging to you, Father.

Resting is an act of faith, a demonstration of trust that God really does have our lives held securely in his hand.

December 4

A soft answer turns away wrath,
but a harsh word stirs up anger.

Proverbs 15:1

Lord, tempers can run short this time of year. Everywhere we go we have to stand in line; most of us feel rushed and stressed, and it's easy to get caught up in the frenetic pace. Make us different this year, Lord! Teach us to use time in line as time to pray, and let us speak and interact with others in a courteous fashion.

No revenge is so honorable as the one not taken.

—Spanish Proverb

December 5

There is no fear in love, but perfect love casts out fear....
We love because he first loved us.

1 John 4:18–19

Father, thank you for initiating our wonderful relationship by loving me first! Your perfect love has taught me to trust you and leave my fear of your judgment behind. Your love for me brings such joy to my life, Lord. Help me spread this joy to others today.

Love is not abstract—it's concrete. It's the reality of self-sacrifice rather than self-preservation, of giving even when it hurts, of forgiving rather than "keeping score."

December 6

*To the only wise God, through Jesus Christ,
to whom be the glory forever!*

Romans 16:27 NIV

ord, so often I believe I know exactly what I think and why, but then I sense your gentle nudging to look at the situation from your perspective. How generous of you to shine your wisdom into the dark corners of my heart and mind! Make me a believer wise in your ways—not one determined to have things my own way.

Integrity without knowledge is weak and useless, and knowledge without integrity is dangerous and dreadful.

—Samuel Johnson

December 7

Jesus Christ is the same yesterday and today and forever.

Hebrews 13:8

ord, what comfort we find in your changeless nature. When we look back and remember all the ways you've guided us in the past, we know we have no need to be anxious about the future. You were, are, and always will be our Savior and Lord. Why should we fear instability when you are always here with us?

Change is a constant part of life, but Jesus is a changeless part of eternity.

December 8

And Mary said, "My soul magnifies the Lord,
and my spirit rejoices in God my Savior."

Luke 1:46–47

When she said these words, Mary was carrying the promised Messiah. The days ahead would not be easy for Mary. How would she explain things to her parents and to Joseph? Was she afraid of how she would be treated by her friends and neighbors, as it would appear that she had been unfaithful? Mary was likely confused and somewhat frightened, but she did not fret. She trusted in the Lord and rejoiced. She praised God for the honor of being chosen to serve him in this unique way.

Father, you've chosen each of us to serve you in unique ways. Help us to embrace the responsibilities and challenges before us as little privileges through which we can faithfully serve you.

December 9

A capable wife who can find? She is far more precious than jewels. The heart of her husband trusts in her, and he will have no lack of gain.

Proverbs 31:10–11

Lord, form me into the best wife and mother I can be. Help me to value what I have and guard my heart from destructive bitterness. Balancing work and home can be challenging, but help me to see

it for the blessing that it is. I have a wonderful, fulfilling life. Distract me when I am tempted to compare my lot with those of others. Help me to remember that one life is not better than any other—they are all simply different. We all have our trials and our blessings, and we all contribute to the world in specific ways.

Love and you shall be loved.

—Ralph Waldo Emerson

December 10

But the tax collector, standing far off, would not even look up to heaven, but was beating his breast and saying, "God, be merciful to me, a sinner!"

Luke 18:13

Lord, on my worst days, I find it comforting to call this parable to mind. On such days I really relate to the tax collector. I feel lost in this world, far from you. Please help me, Lord. Forgive my recent failings and give me the courage, strength, and wisdom to make things right again.

Do not lose courage in considering your own imperfections.

—Francis de Sales

December 11

But the earth will be filled with the knowledge of the glory of the Lord, as the waters cover the sea.

Habakkuk 2:14

Lord, how magnificent is your work on this earth. We can stand at the seashore and feel our own souls rising and filling with your majesty as we marvel at the tides. Or we can walk down a trail and notice that each and every twig has been frosted individually with more icy flakes than we can imagine. We praise you for this awesome creation you share with us, Lord. The more we see of it, the more amazed we are. To you be the glory!

The universe declares your majesty, O Lord, and the song it sings is "Alleluia!"

December 12

And we urge you, brothers and sisters, warn those who are idle and disruptive, encourage the disheartened, help the weak, be patient with everyone.

1 Thessalonians 5:14 NIV

Lord, help us to help each other find you. Help us to encourage each other and to not be too sensitive to constructive criticism. For my part, I ask your forgiveness for all the times I have willingly polluted my mind and spirit by choosing a questionable form of entertainment over a more life-affirming one. Protect me from destructive habits, Lord. I know there are better ways to spend my precious moments on this earth.

Prayer is an aspiration of the heart, it is a simple glance directed toward heaven, it is a cry of gratitude and love in the midst of trial as well as joy.

—Thérèse of Lisieux

December 13

Then [the Lord] said to me, "It is done! I am the Alpha and the Omega, the beginning and the end. To the thirsty I will give water as a gift from the spring of the water of life."

Revelation 21:6

ord, you know all things—from beginning to end—for you are the eternal, all-knowing God. I don't need to fear what is yet to come because I belong to you, and you have given me the gift of eternal life. I come to you today to be refreshed by your presence and your Word.

Don't be afraid of what lies ahead. God will lead his children home safely.

December 14

How very good and pleasant it is when
kindred live together in unity!

Psalm 133:1

ord, time and again I see that you intend for
the generations to go through life together.
The joy the youngest child brings to the eldest
grandparent is such a blessing to all who witness it.
Even when it isn't possible for us all to be together
all the time, let us see the wisdom in sharing our
lives. Please keep us ever alert to the unique gifts each
generation has to share.

When a family
gathers, we see
ourselves reflected
in others, and they
see something of
themselves in us.

December 15

For this is what the high and exalted One says—he who lives forever, whose name is holy: "I live in a high and holy place, but also with the one who is contrite and lowly in spirit, to revive the spirit of the lowly and to revive the heart of the contrite."

Isaiah 57:15 NIV

Lord, in my darkest moments, it is easy to despair and fear that you have given up on me. It would be understandable for you to be angry and disappointed and leave me to my ruin. How comforting it is to know that the minute I regret what I have done and turn to you, you are right where you have been all along—by my side, ready to embrace and carry me until I am strong enough to take a step on my own. Thank you for your faithfulness, Lord—especially when I least deserve it.

After our examination of conscience, we do often find ourselves unlovable, but it is precisely that which makes us want God—because he is the only one who loves the unlovable.

—Fulton Sheen

367

December 16

They shall all know me, from the least of them to the greatest, says the Lord; for I will forgive their iniquity, and remember their sin no more.

Jeremiah 31:34

Lord, if you don't remember our sins, why do we so often beat ourselves up over them? The only possible benefit I can see is that this way, there's less chance that we'll repeat them. But if it be your will, Lord— and to our benefit— grant us your sweet forgetfulness. We accept your gift of

forgiveness, Lord. May we learn to accept your gift of forgetfulness as well.

If only we could grant to ourselves the forgiveness we give to others.

December 17

They are like trees planted by streams of water, which yield their fruit in its season, and their leaves do not wither.

Psalm 1:3

The older I get, the more aware I am of the seasons of life, Lord. I know that when we draw our energy and resources from your living Word, we truly can be compared to the trees that thrive near streams of water. The fruit of a young life lived for you may look a bit different than the fruit visible in the lives of older folks, but it all brings you glory. Thank you, Lord, for supplying your living water through all the seasons of our lives. Without it, we could bear no worthy fruit at all.

I never saw a wild thing sorry for itself

—D. H. Lawrence

December 18

*Therefore be imitators of God, as beloved children,
and live in love, as Christ loved us and gave himself up
for us, a fragrant offering and sacrifice to God.*

Ephesians 5:1–2

Lord, from this past year I'd like to save in
the scrapbook of my life just those days
that brought you glory…days when in spite of my
self-absorption and
often worldly focus, you
were able to accomplish
something through me.
Those are the days I
cherish, Lord. Help me to
move into the next year
more available—more
open—to living such
scrapbook-worthy days.

*Day by day before I sleep,
may I make a memory
God wants to keep.*

December 19

Therefore the Lord himself will give you a sign:
The virgin will conceive and give birth to a son,
and will call him Immanuel.

Isaiah 7:14 NIV

Immanuel—what a beautiful word! It means "God with us." The reality of the birth of Jesus is that he is God, come to be with us, wrapped up in human likeness, and ultimately placed upon a cross as the greatest gift ever given. Now, since his resurrection and ascension, his Spirit remains with us, and we are never alone. Immanuel—God is with us at this very moment.

Jesus, thank you for coming to be with us— for bringing your light into our darkness, your healing to our pain, and your reconciling love to our loneliness.

371

December 20

But when the fullness of time had come,
God sent his Son, born of a woman, born under the
law, in order to redeem those who were under the law,
so that we might receive adoption as children.

Galatians 4:4–5

Father, it's as if time itself was aware of your plan to redeem humanity through your son. In this verse I'm reminded of your perfect timing—that nothing you do is by accident or happenstance. Jesus came at precisely the right time in history to carry out your wonderful purposes. I'll trust you, then, with the timing in my life.

I'll stop fretting and wait patiently. You are in control, and I know you have a plan.

God sees things in light of eternity. His timing may seem
off at times, but in reality, he's always on time.

December 21

And suddenly there was with the angel a multitude
of the heavenly host, praising God and saying,
"Glory to God in the highest heaven, and on earth
peace among those whom he favors!"

Luke 2:13–14

The shepherds got quite a shock that "silent night" as they tended sheep in the hills near Bethlehem. First, an angel gave them a birth announcement of epic proportions. Then, the whole sky lit up with a host of angels who delivered the angelic benediction, "Glory to God in the highest heaven, and on earth peace among those whom he favors!"

Then suddenly, all was silent again. What was the first earthly sound those shepherds heard after this other-worldly encounter? Did a sheep bleat? Did a cricket chirp? What was it like to be there—to be one of the shepherds? What a night!

Father, the events surrounding the birth
of your son send shivers up my spine even
though I've heard them year after year. Thank
you for this time of year, when I can revel in
all the wonder surrounding Jesus' arrival.

December 22

When the angels had left them and gone into heaven, the shepherds said to one another, "Let us go now to Bethlehem and see this thing that has taken place, which the Lord has made known to us."

Luke 2:15

Seeing is believing, right? But from what is recorded of the shepherds' dialogue, it appears that they already believed what the angel told them and were making a beeline to Bethlehem *because* of their belief, not to establish it. What a wonderful faith they had: "Let us...see this thing that has taken place."

Father, I want my faith to be like the shepherds': Not doubting or waffling or wondering if what you say is true, but rather trusting you and taking positive action based on your Word.

December 23

*Mary treasured all these words and
pondered them in her heart.*

Luke 2:19

ary delighted in her son. What an
honor it was to have such an intimate
connection to Jesus. And what a wonderful, loving
mother Mary was! As she listened to the amazing
things the visiting shepherds had to say about her
precious child, Mary quietly
listened, pondering these
things and filing them
away in her heart. May
all mothers look to Mary's
example, Lord. May we
parent generously and
wisely, gently encouraging
our children to look to your
plans for their lives.

*What are Raphael's Madonnas but the shadow of a
mother's love, fixed in permanent outline forever?*

—Thomas Wentworth Higginson

December 24

The people who walked in darkness have seen
a great light; those who lived in a land of deep darkness—
on them light has shined.

Isaiah 9:2

The prophet Isaiah wrote a number of inspired words from God that pointed to the coming of Christ to earth. In this passage, he speaks of a great light shining on those living in a dark land. Spiritual darkness is the deepest kind of darkness. One may live in the darkness of  being physically blind and yet have the light of Christ, which brings meaning, joy, and hope. Without the light of Christ in a life, there is something missing in the soul.

Lord, thank you for filling my life with your light. Though
trials may cast shadows on my soul from time to time,
your light continues to flicker inside of me.

December 25

O come, let us worship and bow down,
let us kneel before the Lord, our Maker!

Psalm 95:6

O Lord, my heart bows down to you this day as surely as if I were kneeling on the ground right beside the shepherds. Thank you, Lord, for exchanging your heavenly glory for an earthly existence so we would have a heavenly existence someday. You, O Lord, are the reason for this joyful time of year. We bow down and praise your holy name.

Miracles are not contrary to nature, but only
contrary to what we know about nature.

—Augustine of Hippo

December 26

And the Word became flesh and lived among us,
and we have seen his glory, the glory as of
a father's only son, full of grace and truth.

John 1:14

Lord, how we love to contemplate your sojourn on earth. How you came that we might see heaven in your eyes even as the earth was beneath your feet. How you were present in the lives of those who walked with you and attentive to the unspoken needs of every heart. How we love to tell of your

sacrifice on the cross so that all of us might one day share eternal life with you. It's the story that never grows old, the only story that has the power to save, the power to transform hearts.

I love to tell the story of unseen things above,
of Jesus and His glory, of Jesus and His love.

—A. Catherine Hankey

December 27

*For a child has been born for us, a son
given to us; authority rests upon his shoulders;
and he is named Wonderful Counselor, Mighty God,
Everlasting Father, Prince of Peace.*

Isaiah 9:6

Jesus fulfilled many roles during his earthly life: son, friend, teacher, and savior. He grappled with many issues—just as we do—but he patiently fulfilled the mission he came to earth to perform. When family friends ran out of wine at the wedding at Cana, Jesus' mother asked him to do something. Jesus hesitated for a moment because he wasn't sure it was time for him to draw such attention to himself, but he soon acquiesced, realizing that his time had, indeed, come. May we follow Jesus' example and always be open to your plans for our lives, Lord.

I praise you, Jesus, for loving us to death—your own death—to offer us the unmatched gift of your saving grace.

December 28

Therefore God also highly exalted him and gave him the name that is above every name, so that at the name of Jesus every knee should bend, in heaven and on earth and under the earth, and every tongue should confess that Jesus Christ is Lord, to the glory of God the Father.

Philippians 2:9–11

Jesus, every time I stop to think of it, I am awed that you provided salvation for us at the price of your own life. Thank you for

opening up the way for me to enjoy eternal life with you. May my being be filled with joy, gratitude, and awe at every mention of your name.

The feeling remains that God is on the journey too.

—Teresa of Avila

December 29

Thanks be to God for his indescribable gift!

2 Corinthians 9:15

ord, how grateful we are that our spirits don't have to sag once the excitement of Christmas is over! We don't want to be like ungrateful children tearing through a pile of presents just to say, "Is that all?" For the gift you gave us at Christmas, your beloved son among us, is a gift that is ours all the days of our lives and throughout eternity! Thank you for the greatest gift of all, Lord.

Jesus is the perfect gift every day of the year.

December 30

The Lord bless you and keep you; the Lord make his face to shine upon you, and be gracious to you; the Lord lift up his countenance upon you, and give you peace.

Numbers 6:24–26

Lord, sometimes it seems as if life is a series of good-byes. I know when I think this way I am focusing on the wrong part, though—for life can also be seen as a series of hellos! Even when the holidays are over and we go back to our regular, day-to-day lives, we come upon beautiful, exciting things every day. We just need to be on the lookout and

ready to accept them into our lives. May I always be ready to accept blessing from you, Lord, whether they are large blessings that bowl me over or small blessings that I might miss if I'm too caught up in my own concerns.

The things that we love tell us what we are.

—Thomas Aquinas

December 31

Continue to live your lives in him, rooted and built up in him and established in the faith, just as you were taught, abounding in thanksgiving.

Colossians 2:6–7

Lord, this time of year is a wonderful time for reflecting over the past year. Sometimes there is pain involved in looking back, but there is also so much joy and so many things that fill our hearts with gratitude. Renew our dedication to living a life that brings you glory for as long as we are on this earth. Remind us of the rich heritage that is ours through you, and keep us both humble and grateful.

A thankful heart is not only the greatest virtue, but the parent of all other virtues.

—Cicero

ACKNOWLEDGMENTS:

Unless otherwise noted, all Scripture quotations are taken from the *New Revised Standard Version* of the Bible. Copyright © 1989 by the Division of Christian Education of the National Council of the Churches of Christ in the United States of America. Used by permission. All rights reserved.

Scripture quotations marked NIV are taken from *The Holy Bible, New International Version*. Copyright © 1973, 1978, 1984, 2011 International Bible Society. Used by permission of Zondervan Publishing House. All rights reserved.

Scripture quotations marked NLT are taken from the *Holy Bible, New Living Translation*. Copyright © 1996. Used by permission of Tyndale House Publishers, Inc., Wheaton, Illinois 60187. All rights reserved.

PHOTO CREDITS:

Front cover: **Shutterstock.com**
Back cover: **Shutterstock.com**

Art Explosion: 160; **Brand X Pictures:** 108, 379; © **Sharon K. Broutzas:** 3, 17, 22, 24, 32, 33, 34, 39, 41, 42, 50, 56, 61, 69, 71, 72, 74, 77, 81, 82, 83, 84, 85, 89, 90, 91, 92, 95, 97, 98, 99, 100, 101, 104, 107, 110, 114, 117, 119, 120, 122, 126, 127, 129, 131, 135, 136, 139, 141, 142, 143, 145, 146, 148, 151, 154, 155, 159, 161, 163, 165, 166, 167, 170, 171, 177, 178, 180, 181, 184, 186, 188, 189, 190, 191, 194, 196, 197, 202, 203, 204, 205, 206, 210, 211, 212, 213, 216, 218, 224, 226, 228, 229, 232, 233, 235, 236, 237, 238, 241, 242, 243, 245, 247, 251, 253, 254, 255, 258, 260, 261, 265, 267, 268, 270, 273, 274, 275, 276, 277, 278, 279, 280, 281, 283, 284, 285, 287, 288, 289, 296, 301, 302, 303, 304, 305, 310, 311, 313, 316, 318, 319, 321, 324, 326, 327, 332, 333, 334, 335, 336, 337, 338, 339, 340, 341, 342, 343, 347, 349, 352, 354, 357, 361, 368, 370, 371, 372, 381, 382; **Corbis:** 149; © **Henry G. Nepomuceno:** 4, 5, 10, 13, 26, 36, 40, 43, 44, 47, 48, 52, 53, 55, 60, 62, 64, 66, 68, 70, 73, 75, 76, 79, 86, 87, 93, 94, 96, 102, 111, 113, 118, 124, 128, 152, 156, 157, 168, 169, 173, 176, 179, 183, 187, 195, 198, 200, 201, 208, 214, 215, 219, 220, 221, 231, 233, 246, 248, 252, 256, 257, 264, 266, 271, 272, 282, 286, 290, 295, 297, 299, 300, 307, 312, 314, 315, 323, 325, 330, 344, 345, 355, 366, 369, 380; **Photodisc:** 15, 23, 27, 31, 35, 37, 38, 45, 49, 51, 65, 80, 103, 105, 109, 115, 123, 125, 130, 133, 137, 140, 147, 150, 172, 174, 192, 217, 239, 240, 244, 250, 259, 263, 269, 291, 298, 308, 322, 331, 351, 353, 373, 378; **PIL Collection:** 25, 234, 359; **Shutterstock.com:** title page, 6, 7, 8, 9, 11, 12, 14, 16, 18, 19, 20, 21, 28, 29, 30, 46, 54, 59, 63, 67, 78, 88, 106, 112, 116, 121, 132, 134, 138, 158, 162, 164, 175, 182, 185, 193, 199, 207, 209, 223, 227, 262, 292, 294, 306, 309, 317, 320, 328, 329, 348, 350, 356, 358, 360, 362, 363, 364, 365, 367, 374, 375, 383; **Thinkstock:** 57, 58, 144, 153, 222, 225, 249, 293, 346, 376, 377